THE MENTORING CORNER

The Mentoring Corner

JORGE LUIS ROMEU

Copyright © 2025 by Jorge Luis Romeu
All rights reserved. No part of this book may be reproduced in any manner whatsoever without written permission except in the case of brief quotations embodied in critical articles and reviews.
First Printing, 2025
cyphrGlyffe, and imprint of Amorphous Publishing Guild
Buffalo, NY USA
www.Amorphous.Press

To all my Brother Freemasons

Contents

Dedication	v
Introduction	1
2014	4
2015	13
2016	34
2017	53
2018	74
2019	95
2020	117
2021	142
2022	167
2023	192
2024	217
2025	244
Abbreviation Guide	264
About the Author	267
Publisher's Note	269

Introduction

I was born in Havana, in 1945, of Cuban and Puerto Rican stock. My father was a lifelong Freemason. I grew up under the Castro government, unfriendly to The Craft and all competing organizations, including Boy Scouts, churches, etc. I joined in 1969, a very difficult time for a young man to become a Mason, due to the burdens the government placed on us. After I left Cuba, in 1980, I joined a Puerto Rican Lodge, and later, one in Upstate New York, where I have lived ever since.

In Puerto Rico, I worked with a small but select group of brothers that edited *ACACIA*, the official Grand Lodge Quarterly, and directed the Bloise Research Lodge. In articles for *ACACIA*, and research papers for Masonic journals and academic proceedings, I discussed issues related to how Brethren participate within The Craft, and to the history of Freemasonry in Cuba, Puerto Rico and Dominican Republic. Such studies helped expand my experiences in Freemasonry, and on how Masons react under different conditions.

When I joined Liverpool Syracuse Lodge, said unusual Masonic trajectory and experiences facilitated my work on Mentoring; first at the Lodge level, and then for Onondaga District, where I became Mentoring Chair and Chairman of the NorthStar Project.

In 2014, I was offered the chance of writing the *Mentor* column for our monthly journal *The Word*, that covers six Masonic districts in Upstate New York. The newspaper was created in 1971 and, after some iterations, became expertly edited by RW Steven Zabriskie. Under his guidance, *The Word* carries the news of all our Lodges, Districts, and Appended Bodies, including Eastern Star; Op-ed pieces such as *Mentor* and *Editor's Prerogative*; and selected historical, ritualistic and esoteric articles from *The Builder*, published a century ago. *The Word* informs Brethren, especially the elderly, shut-ins and winter birds, of what is going on in our Lodges and Districts, as well as providing valuable "food for thought".

The monthly *Mentor* column discusses how current events affect The Craft, and how can we effectively interact with them. For example, we have written about the importance of developing Lodge-Community Activities, in the Sep. 2024, Oct. 2024, Nov. 2024, Dec. 2024, March 2025, and June 2025 issues of *The Word*. We have written about The Craft's Social Philosophy, October 2023; about social activities, Aug. 2016, Sep. 2022 and Membership Issues. We have also written about the great importance of Masonic Journalism, Oct. 2022; and of Media Coverage, June 2022 and April 2025.

We have written about the January 6th 2021 U.S. Capitol Riot, in February, March, April, and June of 2021, from a Masonic perspective, and about the value of Elections Dec. 2022. We have written about how Freemasonry, with its tenets of Tolerance and Brotherly Love, can help defuse our Toxic Divisions, and about how, by developing community projects, The Craft can help offset them, in the Jan. 2022, Feb. 2022, March 2024 issues. We have also written several articles providing an overview of the history of Freemasonry in Cuba, in the XIX Century and the XX Century.

We come from a Spanish Caribbean Freemasonry background, which is more action-oriented than the American one, perhaps because in the US many social functions (education, welfare, etc.) are successfully developed by the government — and in the Spanish Caribbean these are not. There, The Craft has worked hard to fill said void. And their community action approach has helped enhance its public image, and thence its recruitment and retention. We believe that a proactive Craft, that engages with community issues in a non-political manner, may attract and retain additional members to its ranks.

Finally, there is one important dimension linked to our journalistic endeavors and our newspaper *The Word*: its historical value. The word portrays the Masonic endeavors of a mostly rural, but essentially American segment of our society. And it has done this for about half a century.

Perhaps, sometime in the future, some Masonic historians will have an interest in studying Masonic behavior during this very interesting period we are currently living in our country. And perhaps they will seek in our newspaper, as we seek today in *The Builder*, the necessary research material to investigate what were the most important issues of our time, how these were developed throughout the years, and who were the key movers and shakers in Grand Lodge, and in its Lodges.

And perhaps our newspaper *The Word*, and our *Mentor* columns, will provide them with some answers.

2014

The Mentoring Corner, Initial Column
The Word, 18 September 2014

    Hello, Brothers! I am the new Mentoring Chair for the District. I am honored with this important task, and plan to follow in the foot-steps of my predecessor, Bro. Gabriel Iza (who wrote our Mentoring Manual). I also look forward to each Lodge's Mentoring officer's input and suggestions on what has worked for them, or has not. We don't want to re-invent the wheel!

    Mentoring is a very important activity, as it seriously impacts retention of newly raised Brothers. It has at least three important components: Protocol, Liturgy, and Social. Every new member needs to learn how to deal with our ceremony Protocol, which is most likely new and different to them. Very important is for them to understand what meaning such ceremonies convey, as Freemasonry's method of teaching is through images. Finally, the newly-raised Brothers need to quickly feel at home in their new Lodges, and to know their Lodge Brethren.

We look forward to visiting the District Lodges with our DDGM, and to getting in contact and working with our Lodge Mentoring officers, to accomplish this task.

Fraternally/Jorge.

Jorge L. Romeu, MM
Onondaga District Mentoring Chair.
Liverpool Syracuse Lodge No. 501

The Mentoring Corner

The Word, 8 October 2014

Hello, Brothers! Just a short follow up on our Mentoring activities. We have been visiting some of our District Lodges with the DDGM, meeting some of you, and leaving my email and phone (which are also included below) in case you want to contact me.

We have mentioned in such visits how Mentoring activity is different from Masonic Education. Mentoring takes place during the crucial first year of newly raised Brothers' Lodge life, and can seriously impact their retention. Masonic Education is a lifelong endeavor, and builds upon that.

One of the first questions that we may deal with, during Mentoring, pertains to explaining what is a Mason. For, many of our newly raised Brothers may not have a clear idea of what we are, or stand for. There are many explanations, all of them very correct. But I prefer Brother George H. Free's poem: *What Makes a Mason?* which begins and continues as follows:

What makes you a MASON, o Brother of Mine? It isn't the duegard nor is it the sign...

That you to your sworn obligation are true –'Tis that, Brother mine, makes a Mason of you...

The entire poem can be found in http://www.masonic-world.com/education/files/feb03/nov.htm [link no longer active; full poem below]

Fraternally/Jorge.

Jorge L. Romeu, MM
Onondaga District Mentoring Chair.
Liverpool Syracuse Lodge No. 501

What Makes A Man A Mason?

{A Poem by George M. Free, widely available across the Internet, but little information can be found about its author or when written}

What makes a man a Mason, O brother of mine?
It isn't the due guard, nor is it the sign,
It isn't the jewel which hangs on your breast
It isn't the apron in which you are dressed

It isn't the step, nor the token, nor the grip,
Nor lectures that fluently flow from the lip,
Nor yet the possession of that mystic word
On five points of fellowship duly conferred.

Though these are essential, desirable, fine,
They don't make a Mason, O brother of mine.
That you to your sworn obligation are true
'Tis that, brother mine, makes a Mason of you.

Secure in your heart you must safeguard and trust,
With lodge and with brother be honest and just,
Assist the deserving who cry in their need,
Be chaste in your thought, in your word and your deed.

Support he who falters, with hope banish fear,
And whisper advice in an erring one's ear.
Then will the Great Lights on your path brightly shine,
And you'll be a Mason, O brother of mine.

Your use of life's hours by the gauge you must try,
The gavel of vices with courage apply;
Your walk must be upright, as shown by the plumb,
On the level, to bourn whence no travelers come,
The Book of your faith be the rule and the guide,

The compass your passions shut safely inside;
The stone which the Architect placed in your care
Must pass the strict test of His unerring square.
And then you will meet with approval divine,
And you'll be a Mason, O brother of mine.

The Mentoring Corner

November 2014

Hello, Brothers!

Our Institution has many facets, and allows us to develop different interests in it. For, Freemasonry is like a mirror: you get out of it, just as much as you put into it.

A new Brother may already have, in his mind, a specific objective to achieve. For example, he may seek Fellowship, which is very legitimate. Or he may look for self-improvement, or esoteric knowledge. But Freemasonry offers much more! As mentors, we should discover these specific objectives, and help our new Brother to accomplish them. And we should also show him, how to achieve so many other goals that our Institution inspires.

Our MW Grand Master W. J. Thomas ended his St. John's Day speech, in Utica, quoting from the poem The Builders (http://www.ellenbailey.com/poems/ellen_152.htm) [link no longer available; full version follows]:

> Am I a builder who works with care
> Measuring life by the rule and square;
> Or am I a wrecker as I walk the town
> Content with the labor of tearing down?

For, through its ethical component, Freemasonry helps build better men and citizens, stronger families and friendships, fruitful communities, and fuller lives.

Fraternally/Jorge.

Jorge L. Romeu, MM
Liverpool Syracuse Lodge No. 501
Onondaga District Mentoring Chair

A Builder or a Wrecker

{By Edgar "Eddie" A. Guest (1881-1959)}

As I watched them tear a building down
A gang of men in a busy town
With a ho-heave-ho, and a lusty yell
They swung a beam and the side wall fell
I asked the foreman, "Are these men skilled,
And the men you'd hire if you wanted to build?"
He gave a laugh and said, "No, indeed,
Just common labor is all I need."
"I can easily wreck in a day or two,
What builders have taken years to do."

And I thought to myself, as I went my way
Which of these roles have I tried to play?
Am I a builder who works with care,
Measuring life by rule and square?
Am I shaping my work to a well-made plan
Patiently doing the best I can?
Or am I a wrecker who walks to town
Content with the labor of tearing down?
"O Lord let my life and my labors be
That which will build for eternity!"

The Mentoring Corner
December 2014

Hello, Brothers!

I received an interesting question (and they are most welcome!). Who can be a Mentor? First, there should be at least two. One is the Brother who introduces the candidate. He can acquaint the new Brother with other Lodge members, sit with him in Lodge, and explain to him what is happening, and what to do, when. The second Mentor deals with the significance of our Ritual and our Craft. And the case can be made for selecting, as Mentor, a relatively novel Brother.

When instruction happens, the teacher usually learns as much as the student. The novel Mentor has an opportunity to fix and expand on what he has, himself, learned. He also has a more recent experience about what a candidate, or a newly raised Brother, encounters after joining our Institution. The novel Mentor should regularly consult an older, and more experienced Brother. And above all, he must READ! For there are certain books the Mentor must review.

First, is the "Standard Work and Lectures of Ancient Craft Masonry" (the little black book). Then, the MDC booklet that, most likely, the novel Mentor has studied, himself. Then, is the Mentoring Guide that VW Gabe Iza carefully prepared: every Lodge in our District has a copy. Finally, there is a jewel of a book: "The Builders" (http://sacred-texts.com/mas/bui/index.htm), written one century ago by Bro. Joseph F. Newton, Grand Chaplain of the Grand Lodge of Iowa. It remains very current and instructive, and has an excellent and complete discussion of the history of our Institution. One can borrow "The Builders" (and other books) from our own Chancellor Livingston Library (http://www.nymasoniclibrary.org/), or buy it from Macoy (http://www.macoy.com/)

Finally, if a Mentoring team combining a novel and an experienced Brother is formed, it is even better!

Fraternally/Jorge.

Jorge L. Romeu, MM
Liverpool Syracuse Lodge No. 501
Onondaga District Mentoring Chair

2015

The Mentoring Corner

January 2015

Hello, Brothers!

We have been talking about ideas to implement with new petitioners, Entered Apprentices, Fellow Craftsmen, and Raised Brothers, to combat attrition and help them in their first steps toward becoming good Masons. Notwithstanding all things already said, there is one that stands out, and that has been raised time and again throughout the years by many Brethren, including our own Grand Master William J. Thomas: *Avoiding Boring Lodge Meetings!*

Reasons for Boring meetings, as well as ideas to enrich them have been identified in many books and articles (e.g. "About Time": http://www.msana.com/aboutime_foreword.asp) [page unavailable]*, as well as opinions, from developing new ideas (e.g. "A Pilgrim s Path", by Bro. John J. Robinson), to better implementing older ones (e.g. PGM Dwight L. Smith's "Withering are we Traveling", in: http://pictoumasons.org/library/

Smith,%20Dwight%20L%20~%20WhitherAreWeTraveling%20%5Bpdf%5D.pdf [site unavailable]* and "Why This Confusion?", also available in the Internet: http://masonicrestorationfoundation.org/documents/DLS_WhyThisConfusion.pdf. All of them present and illustrate very interesting, valid and persuasive points of view.

Some ideas include developing a Bank of Speakers in our Districts, available to all Lodges; or inviting outside speakers, to develop interesting topics. Drawbacks include difficulties in finding skilled speakers with appropriate subjects that will interest most lodge members.

Liverpool Syracuse Lodge has successfully used the Question Box. A box is placed in the foyer, where anonymous questions are submitted. At the end of each meeting, questions are introduced, then resolved by general participation. Seasoned brethren enjoy sharing their knowledge about the issue at hand, while novice ones enjoy acquiring more Light in Masonry. Everyone gains.

Whatever the approach, it is definitely necessary to make Lodge Meetings interesting: not only to keep in the new members, but also to raise attendance among the old ones! Interesting lodge meetings build stronger lodges and better-educated Masons. They also build a stronger Craft.

Fraternally/Jorge.

Jorge L. Romeu, MM
Liverpool Syracuse Lodge No. 501
Onondaga District Mentoring Chair

*"IT'S ABOUT TIME! Moving Masonry into the 21st Century" by the Masonic Information Center, and Dwight L. Smith's "Withering are

we Traveling" and *"Why This Confusion?"*, *are available as a PDF online*

The Mentoring Corner

February 2015

Hello, Brothers!

As Mentors, we often receive these questions: What is Freemasonry? What are its aims and objectives? What does it do? We want to share two points of view that address them: one from within our own Craft, and another from outside of it.

PGM Bro. Dwight L. Smith, in his book Whither are we Traveling, answered it: Freemasonry erects its temples within the hearts of men. Our own Declaration of Principles proclaims: Through the improvement and strengthening of the character of the individual man, Freemasonry seeks to improve the community. Then, PGM Smith added: The purpose of Freemasonry is to take an individual one man at a time and try to make a better man out of him.

Bro. Smith also quoted Venerable Bro. Nathan Roscoe Pound, Deputy Grand Master for the Grand Lodge of Massachusetts, and Dean of Harvard s Law School. Bro. Roscoe Pound, in his message to the Craft, considered that Freemasonry has more to offer the Twentieth Century than the Twentieth Century has to offer Freemasonry.

An independent point of view is advanced by Prof. Jose A. Ferrer Benimeli, who is not a Mason but a Jesuit researcher. Ferrer Benimeli, who founded and chaired CEHME, a European Center for the Study of Masonic History, considers that

Freemasonry is an association that defends human dignity, solidarity and fraternity. Its objective is to obtain the moral and cultural improvement of its members, through the construction of a symbolic temple dedicated to virtue. ... It is a reunion of men that believe in God, and work together over differences in social rank, and diversity in political and religious opinions. http://www.aragoninvestiga.org/tag/centro-de-estudios-historicos-de-la-masoneria-espanola/ [page unavailable]

Sometime soon, we plan to convene a meeting with all Mentoring or Education Officers, from our Onondaga District Lodges, to overview and implement the excellent Mentoring Handbook that VW Bro. Gabe Iza prepared, when he was the District Mentoring Chair.

Fraternally/Jorge.

Jorge L. Romeu, MM
Liverpool Syracuse Lodge No. 501
Onondaga District Mentoring Chair

The Mentoring Corner

March 2015

Hello, Brothers!

We want to probe further into three important questions regarding the nature of Freemasonry. We share an address given by Bro. Laurence Healey, Senior Grand Warden of the Grand Lodge of British Columbia (http://freemasonry.bcy.ca/grand_mas-

THE MENTORING CORNER ~ 17

ters/healey_l/service_club.html) and delivered to the 10th Annual Conference of Western Canadian Grand Lodges, in response to the important question: "Should Our Grand Lodges Sponsor a Specific Program?"

Bro. Healy addresses a topic often raised by some brethren: *why doesn't the Craft directly put its principles into practice through specific social or community projects?* Its answer may help better understand what is Freemasonry, what are its aims and objectives, and what does it do.

Bro. Healy explains how.

> In the masonic design the major effort is directed toward the development of character and improvement of life and conduct in the individual man ... By a peculiar system of ritual and ceremonies, great principles of morality and virtue are inculcated. ... Lessons are derived from the powerful drama of life and death as portrayed in its allegories ... keeping the great principles of Truth, Honor, Charity and Justice strong and active in the lives of individuals.

Bro. Healy concludes that Freemasonry deals in principles rather than in projects, in the dissemination of ideals rather than in programs of self-advertisement. Then, he provides this image:

> A masonic lodge may be likened to a school, or university. ... Its graduates, having learned that Freemasonry is a way of life, a quality of life to be lived day by day, go out into the world and give practical effect to the principles and ideals which they have acquired.

By the time *The Word* issue appears, we will have scheduled a meeting with all Mentoring or Education Officers, from our Onondaga District Lodges, to discuss the Mentoring Handbook that Bro. Iza prepared. Mentoring is so important that it is discussed on page 130 of the "24 Inch Gauge, the Masonic Resource Guide" used in the *Road to the East* course, which is taken by all those interested in becoming Lodge Wardens and Masters.

Fraternally/Jorge.

Jorge L. Romeu, MM
Liverpool Syracuse Lodge No. 501
Onondaga District Mentoring Chair

The Mentoring Corner

April 2015

Hello, Brothers!

A Brother asks us what other activities, in addition to attending Lodge and building our character, can we undertake as Freemasons. Indeed, *in the masonic design the major effort is directed toward development of character*. This is our main objective, from which everything else stems. However, from the application of this tenant, and of our principles of *Truth, Honor, Charity and Justice*, many additional outcomes such as Fellowship and Community Commitment are derived. And interested Brethren are encouraged to participate.

Members of other organizations also make good friends. But, the sharing of our ethical principles and values make those we interact with, in Lodge, something special: Brothers. Such strong bonding provides many opportunities to create diverse, interesting and useful activities.

A second, important result of Freemasonry stems from its purpose of *making some Good men Better*. For, some of these better men may feel a call to contribute to their community, and will do so in many ways. For example, we can, silently and individually, visit the sick, volunteer as school tutors or library storytellers, or create our own service projects, like the one this mentor develops: http://web.cortland.edu/matresearch.

We can also work in some of our particular Lodge formal community programs, such as Visits with Santa, Easter Eggs Hunt, etc.. Or we can participate in Grand Lodge-fostered programs such as blood donations and pantry drives, or in our Masonic Child ID, among several others.

New programs can be discussed among interested Brethren, before and after our Lodge sessions. Relevant ones can then be implemented by our Lodge, or developed elsewhere. Bro. Mark Tabbert, in his book "American Freemasons" (page 163), describes how clubs like Rotarians and Kiwanis were originally organized by Freemasons, looking to implement their new ideas.

Our Craft, acting as a catalyst agent, has traditionally stimulated and linked Brethren interested in community service. Bro. Angel Millar, in his book Freemasonry: a history, states how to some degree American Masonry has remained polarized ... between essentially civic and community-based, and mystical (p. 219). Bros. Washington and Franklin are examples.

In every case, however, we must be very careful that our proposals do not disrupt the *Lodge Harmony*. For, *Harmony is the support of all Institutions, especially that of ours*.

Fraternally/Jorge.

Jorge L. Romeu, MM
Liverpool Syracuse Lodge No. 501
Onondaga District Mentoring Chair

The Mentoring Corner

May 2015

Hello, Brothers!

Today, I would like to talk again about Fellowship. But not only about that one which we keep with our own Lodge Brothers; I would like to talk about the Fellowship we keep with Brothers we never met before, but who also belong to our International Fraternity.

I am writing these lines while doing the night shift for my ailing son, in the cancer ward of the Johns Hopkins Hospital, in Baltimore (what an Institution! Not enough words to praise it!). We hastily prepared our trip. I put the Masonic emblem on my coat lapel and emailed my Mentor, asking for his help and his advice. He contacted GLMD, and found a Brother that would meet with me, as I got there.

These days, when many of us have health insurance, disability benefits, etc., material support is not what we most need. A friendly smile and a listening ear are thoroughly appreciated. Grand Chaplain sought us and prayed with us, and offered his house for us to rest, between shifts. We talked about things, both my wife and I feared, and were unable to discuss among ourselves.

In the next few days, I had several positive experiences. In the hospital X-ray room, a nurse saw my emblem and asked me: "Are you a Mason?"

"Yes, I am", I said.

"My Grand-daddy was also a Mason."

"He must have been a good man", I said.

She asked for my cell phone number: "Go back to your room. I will let you know when your son is done. No point in waiting here."

Even after they have gone to the Eternal East, some Brothers are still helpful. Her Grandfather was.

One can easily identify, in a cancer ward, a family member in distress. If a person is not a doctor, nurse or staff (easily recognized by their white, green or blue uniform), or a patient, dragging a rolling tree, and connected to all sorts of I.V. bags and lines, then one is a family caregivers. No sign of distress is necessary in those circumstances, for a Mason to help out, as several did. A staff approached me in a corridor: I am a Prince Hall , he said. Can I be of assistance? I just said: Oh, my Brother, Very gently, he took me to the cafeteria for a long and affectionate talk.

That night, during my long shift, I looked up Maryland's Prince Hall Grand Lodge. Its web page has an excellent discussion on why should anyone consider becoming a Mason, posing questions such as: do you believe that you have a responsibility to leave the world a better place than you found it, and that it is not only more blessed to give than to receive, but also more fun? The entire questionnaire is available in http://www.mwphglmd.org/How-To-Join.html

Fraternally/Jorge.

Jorge L. Romeu, MM
Liverpool Syracuse Lodge No. 501
Onondaga District Mentoring Chair

The Mentoring Corner

June 2015

Hello, Brothers!

I am going over some of my Mentoring material, while doing the night shift in the Johns Hopkins Hospital, in Baltimore. And I have found a very interesting and valid question that a New Brother has sent me: why do we place such importance in learning by heart our Ritual? Indeed, some of us have, at some time or another, posed ourselves a similar question. The standard answer is that Ritual is the way our Institution uses to communicate its teachings. But we can certainly go further than that.

There are two ways to deal with the Ritual. We can repeat its words quickly, to get it over. Or we can say them slowly, as we think them through. The latter way is very productive, as indeed, every part of the Ritual communicates an important lesson from our Institution.

One way to make our Lodge Sessions more interesting and interactive, as suggested by our recently re-elected Grand Master Thomas, would be to ask Brethren to state which part of the Ritual they like best, and why. This would generate a very lively and instructive discussion.

For example, I prefer the Ritual section of closing the Lodge in the Third Degree. The Master, from his Station, asks the Senior Warden a question. The Senior Warden then answers it and all, officers and Brethren, descend to the common level of the Lodge.

I believe that interacting *On the Level* is one of the strongest values instilled by our Fraternity!

Throughout the time we have had, and we continue to have in our days, many important or famous Brothers. Some of them have obtained distinguished college degrees, have performed relevant feats, or have held high-ranking government or private sector positions. Others of us are good family men, who attend Lodge regularly. But in Lodge, we all meet On the Level. No one is addressed as Doctor, General, Mayor, or Governor. We use, instead, the highest title that we can have: *Brother*.

In 1717, when the first Grand Lodge was founded in London and monarchy prevailed, with its titles, privileges and hierarchies, the concept of assessing the significance of an individual by his character and personal merit, not his wealth or status in society, was (and still is) a revolutionary concept. Prof. Margaret Jacob, a Masonic historian and scholar from UCLA, has defined our Institution as a school of Government. Her excellent book "Living the Enlightenment", on the beginnings of Freemasonry, is available in the Masonic History reading course of our Grand Lodge's Chancellor Livingston Library and can be requested by mail at no cost.

Fraternally/Jorge.

Jorge L. Romeu, MM
Liverpool Syracuse Lodge No. 501

Onondaga District Mentoring Chair

The Mentoring Corner
September 2015

Hello, Brothers!

As I write these lines, we are back in Syracuse. Our son is gone, after five long months of suffering in hospitals and hospices. As Masons, we believe in God, who Giveth and Taketh Away. God gave us the opportunity to care for him day and night throughout his ordeal and for him to have the best medical care possible. As Masons, we believe in an afterlife, where he is now, and from where he can oversee and perhaps help his teen-ager boy. So Mote it Be!

Life continues, so we proceed with our Mentoring work. Starting with this issue, we will talk about the content included in the sections of our excellent District Mentoring Manual. And we will strive to make it fit within the new Mentoring guidelines that our GLNY has now created.

Firstly, we ask every Lodge Master to assign (if it doesn't already exist) a Mentoring Officer, possibly different from the Education Officer, in every Lodge. And then to avail this officer with the Mentoring Manual that has already been sent to every Lodge. If any Lodge does not have a Manual, please get in contact with us, to provide them with one.

Then, we will have a meeting with all Mentoring Officers, at the end of October, to go over the material in the Manual (after every Mentoring Officer has taken a look at it on their own).

We are hoping to have every new Brother, this year, follow the Mentoring sequence described in the Manual. This will not only help educate our new Brethren, but also will help the older ones to refresh things Masonic. The procedure would work this way:

Our dream Mentoring Team would be composed of four Brothers. The Brother who signed the Petition will introduce the new Brother to other Lodge members and will sit with him during his first Lodge sessions, instructing him on the procedures. Then, there will be two other Brothers, one more senior in the Lodge and the other more recently raised. They will meet and discuss the Mentoring Manual material with our new Brother. Difficult questions would be answered by the more senior one, or brought up to the Lodge for further Light, so no errors are introduced.

This procedure allows four Lodge members to learn or review Masonic issues. If each Lodge raises five new members, in five years all active Lodge members would have had an opportunity to participate, learning new, or reviewing material that they may have seen a long time ago.

We look forward to visiting our District Lodges with the DDGM Official Family the following weeks and to address questions and suggestions that any Brother may have regarding these ideas.

Fraternally/Jorge.

Jorge L. Romeu, MM
Liverpool Syracuse Lodge No. 501
Onondaga District Mentoring Chair

The Mentoring Corner

October 2015

{THIS COLUMN WAS SUPERSEDED BY THE NEXT ONE. IT WAS NEVER PUBLISHED.}

Hello, Brothers!

By the time you read these lines, the Onondaga District Mentoring Officers will have had a meeting to discuss the material in our Mentoring Manual. Lodge Masters have been asked to name a Mentoring Officer, possibly different from their Education Officer, in every Lodge. Masters should avail this officer with the Mentoring Manual that was sent to every Lodge. If any Lodge still does not have such Manual, please contact us to obtain it. In this article, we will briefly comment on pages 2 through 6, of the first section of the Manual.

Mentoring purpose is to provide the newly raised Brother with some basic information about our Institution's laws, obligations and activities, as well as his basic rights, privileges, and duties. It is more than teaching the letter of these topics; it is about conveying the Spirit of Freemasonry, of its key purposes, and ideals. In particular, Mentors should present a brief History of Masonry and discuss questions such as: What is Masonry? and What have thou come here to do?

Such topics will be explored further in the Masonic Development Course (MDC), discussed in Lodge, and through the readings done during the Masonic career of the new Brother.

The Goals of the Mentoring Program include developing fellowship and interest, commitment and enthusiasm, get them involved in Lodge life, and unlock their potential to become leaders.

The Program consists of a series of meetings between Mentor(s) and the new Brother, starting just after he has signed his Petition, and ending one year later. A Mentor can be any Master Mason, responsible for providing the new Brother with a solid foundation in the Craft. He will become a wise, faithful advisor, a friend and a teacher. Probably the single and most important qualification of a Mentor is the desire and willingness to become one, as well as the commitment to follow through, and to read and investigate further the material he is teaching.

Duties of a Mentor include preparing himself, and then regularly meeting the new Member in an atmosphere of warmth and informality that encourages questions and raises interest. Also, a good Mentor monitors the comfort level and involvement in Lodge of the new Member, and fills in any perceived gap that may prevent or delay his active participation in Lodge life.

We look forward to continuing to overview the Mentoring Manual for those who were not able to participate in our meetings, as well as to visit our District Lodges during the DDGM OV [Official Visit], and address any questions that our Brothers may have, regarding these Mentoring issues readings.

Fraternally/Jorge.

Jorge L. Romeu, MM
Liverpool Syracuse Lodge No. 501
Onondaga District Mentoring Chair

The Mentoring Corner

October 2015

Hello, Brothers!

Friday night we had our Onondaga District Grand Lecturer s Convention. Our Grand Lecturer, RW Richard Kessler, presented and commented many informative facets of the Ritual of the Entered Apprentice Degree. There were over 100 Brethren present from every lodge in the district!

During the Convention, I was informed about how our Deputy Grand Master has developed a new Mentoring Program (see the Fall Issue of The Empire State Masons, page 9). The DGM's new mentoring program is called the *Northstar Program*, and will be introduced in the MidState region very soon, most likely prior to Christmas.

Of course, if there is a general Mentoring Program, this is the one that should be implemented. Thence, I will stop our current District mentoring efforts until we receive the DGM s Mentoring Program and find out more about it, so that we can start implementing it in Onondaga District.

The meeting of all Lodge Mentoring Officers convened for the end of October is now deferred, until we receive information and instructions from Grand Lodge, regarding the new Northstar Program and its implementation.

This new development only underlines the great importance that Mentoring has, and how our Masonic district was moving in the right direction.

However, we can still take some preliminary steps in each lodge. For, Lodges will still need:

1) To identify a candidate for Mentoring Officer, in each Lodge.

2) To identify a Group of Master Masons, willing and able to volunteer as Mentors

All these candidates and volunteers should need to begin reviewing background materials, such as the MDC booklet and the Standard Work and Lectures of the Grand Lodge of New York.

Fraternally/Jorge.

Jorge L. Romeu, MM
Liverpool Syracuse Lodge No. 501
Onondaga District Mentoring Chair

The Mentoring Corner
November 2015

Hello, Brothers!

We have already said how our GLNY Deputy Grand Master has developed the new Northstar Mentoring Program, which will be introduced in the Mid-State region very soon. Our DDGM RW Ed Sinay will tell us more about this during the Training on December 12th.

To better prepare ourselves, we can take some preliminary steps in each lodge. We can identify a candidate for Mentoring Officer, as well as some Master Masons, willing and able to volunteer as Mentors. All these candidates and volunteers may begin reviewing background materials, such as the MDC booklet and the *Standard Work and Lectures* of the Grand Lodge of New York.

Meanwhile, I would like to share a recent and interesting experience. I attended an Academic conference on History of Latin American Freemasonry at the University of Costa Rica: http://www.ivsimposiohistoriamasoneriaucr.blogspot.com/

Several academic historians (some of which also belong to our Institution) took part, presenting on Freemasonry in Costa Rica, Mexico, Argentina, Chile, Cuba, and Puerto Rico, among other countries. But the most important feature was how, the Grand Master of the Grand Lodge of Costa Rica, and the Chancellor of the University of Costa Rica, signed a Memorandum of Agreement to conduct joint activities, including research on Freemasonry.

This is not new, nor unique. The Grand Lodge of California and UCLA have had such agreement and have conducted joint activities, including developing an international research conference in 2011, in Los Angeles. Some of the research papers produced in such conference were published in the journal REHMLAC, and are available in the Internet: http://www.history.ucla.edu/news-old/professor-jacob-highlighted-in-academic-journal [page unavailable]

It is good that academics (and the general public) are interested in the history of our Institution. And if so, it is good that Grand Lodges become part of this movement, to provide the correct and complete information to interested academics.

Fraternally/Jorge.

Jorge L. Romeu, MM
Liverpool Syracuse Lodge No. 501
Onondaga District Mentoring Chair

The Mentoring Corner

December 2015

Hello, Brothers!

By the time you read these lines, a group of about forty of us will have already received the *Success Coach Training Seminar* for the **NorthStar Project**. Our Deputy Grand Master and the Membership Development Committee, with the support and approbation of our Grand Master, have developed the project and its seminar, which was offered for several CNY Masonic Districts on December 12th at Memorial Lodge, North Syracuse.

NorthStar addresses some current membership issues the Craft is facing, by strengthening the process of selection and the vetting of candidates, as well as by mentoring them as they progress through their degrees. This way, NorthStar deals with two important issues: putting more men into Masonry and putting more Masonry into men. The reader can find more information in the current (Winter) issue of *The Empire State Mason* (see the article on pages 4 and 5).

Meanwhile, I will share some very useful thoughts we found in the book "Mentoring 101" (by John C. Maxwell; Ed. Thomas Nelson) that a dear Brother pointed out to me. Some of these are:

Mentoring is not something that most people learn in school.

The more you understand people, the greater your chance of success in mentoring.

As you prepare to develop others, ask them to share their story with you.

Go into the process expecting nothing but personal satisfaction.

Some obstacles created by mentors: lack of clear direction; poor communication

Pay less attention to what men say; but watch what they do.

Without leadership there is no teamwork; leadership is influence.

Leaders share two things: they are going somewhere, and can persuade others to go.

Some people seem to hinder you; others add value to you — choose the latter.

Two kinds of leaders: those who attract followers, and those who attract other leaders.

Focus on other people s strengths, and not on their weaknesses.

It is always better to share power, instead of holding to power.

Nothing is more powerful than an idea whose time has come.

Get people around you who can inspire you with their ideas.

THE MENTORING CORNER ~ 33

You can go as fast as the slowest person, or as far as the weakest.

Commitment is the key to success in every aspect of life.

The person who succeeds has a program that goes straight to its goal.

Lack of loyalty is the key to ruining your relationship with others.

Fraternally/Jorge.

Jorge L. Romeu, MM
Liverpool Syracuse Lodge No. 501
Onondaga District Mentoring Chair

2016

The Mentoring Corner

January 2016

Hello, Brothers!

The one-day NorthStar Seminar took place at Memorial Lodge, North Syracuse, on December 12th and it was a complete success! Over fifty Brothers, representing Lodges from most Central New York Districts, received instruction on both parts of NorthStar: the Candidate Selection Process, and Successful Coaching. The latter one is closer to our old district Mentoring program — but it is good for our entire Grand Lodge to have a unified material. Selection Process is a welcome improvement, as it develops several meetings with a presumptive candidate and his family, before handing him the Petition. This way, we explore whether our Fraternity is a good match for him, and he for our Fraternity, thus saving much frustration and a potential attrition.

Our current attrition rates are high — but this is not exclusive of our Grand Lodge. In the article *The Heart of the Craft* (Page 49 of the March issue of *The Square*, a British independent magazine for Freemasons) author John M. Grange states "around 100 Lodges are closing each year over the last decade; ... almost a third of new members leaving within five years". And on Page 61 of that same issue, we read the article Investing in the Growth of the Brotherhood, by Robert A. Shively, Exec. Dir. of Kansas Masonic Foundation. Bro Shively states how: "Steady membership declines threaten the sustainability of fraternal organizations nationwide". He then describes the Member survey they have developed, and dwells on its results and conclusions.

Closer to home, Florida PGM J. Aladro, in his book "Are We Making Good Men Better?" (http://www.amazon.com/Are-Making-Good-Men-Better/dp/0996306633) discusses important issues that we need to stress in Masonic Education and develops an entire chapter on Mentoring.

Yours truly is an incorrigible optimist. Maybe the current attrition situation is a blessing in disguise. Maybe we needed to purge our ranks and, instead of adding more men into Masonry, we should be adding more Masonry into men. NorthStar Mentoring Program may just do that!

Firstly, the entire process slows down (maybe we are just going too fast in selecting and in raising poorly prepared Brethren). This gives the candidates more time to reflect on what they are about to do, as well as to better process and understand the three degrees they are receiving.

In addition, if Mentoring teams are composed of at least two members (one seasoned and one recently raised Brother), they can also become tools for refreshing and strengthening some material already seen, but so important that it might prove an excellent idea to review!

I take the opportunity to wish you all, a happy, healthy, and productive New Year!
Fraternally/Jorge.

Jorge L. Romeu, MM
Onondaga District Mentoring Chair

The Mentoring Corner

February 2016

Hello, Brothers!

We have enthusiastically started implementing the **North-Star** program in our Lodge. We have started meeting with our new prospect candidates, to follow all the steps in the Candidate Selection Process before handing them the petition. And we plan to follow all the steps in the *Successful Coaching* part, after their Initiation.

The mentoring or second section of NorthStar (*Successful Coaching*) has many common features with older mentoring manuals such as LSOME or our own district Mentoring Manual (and could be used by future mentors to complement their review of the materials in NorthStar). However, by using NorthStar as a common manual to instruct our new Brothers, we will all be on the same page, thus avoiding the risk of leaving important areas without being covered, or of covering too much on other areas and topics that could better be done at a later stage.

The initial section of NorthStar (*Candidate Selection Process*) seems, in our opinion, more crucial. Such was not done before (or if it was done, it was less emphasized). It pertains to establishing whether the prospective candidate is a good match for our Insti-

THE MENTORING CORNER ~ 37

tution, and whether Freemasonry is a good match for him. If either is not, then it is better not to proceed with the Petition. We may end with the new Brother dropping his membership in the Lodge, shortly after.

Avoiding such situations will help in reducing our current attrition rates two-fold: we will avoid having one less brother — and we will avoid having a disenchanted individual, perhaps not offering the best of assessments of our Craft out there, thus influencing others.

We have again found the topic of attrition discussed in several articles of the December 2015 issue of *The Square* (http://www.thesquaremagazine.com/). Bro. David Cameron, of the GL of Ontario, Canada, shares his thoughts about where Freemasonry is going — or should be going (page20). Bro David Cons, PPGM for Middlesex, England, shares his thoughts about what Freemasonry has to offer to those who join us. Bro. Alex Lishanin reflects on how he became a Mason, and what it means to him and to others he met in the process. PGM Aladro, asks: are we, as Masons, having an identity crisis?" (Masonic Discourses http://www.amazon.com/Masonic-Discourses-Volume-Educated-Dedicated/dp/0989556360 page 81). We could use articles such as these, from recent masonic literature, to generate lively conversations in our Lodge sessions!

For those who were unable to attend the NorthStar training on December 12th, and are still interested in finding out more about it, we will be giving a one-hour overview presentation at Liverpool Syracuse Lodge No. 501, on Wednesday, March 16th, at 7 pm.

Fraternally/Jorge.

Jorge L. Romeu
Onondaga District Mentoring Chair

The Mentoring Corner

March 2016

Hello, Brothers!

We have been reading different comments about the importance of the Ritual lately. And this is an extremely important topic for Mentoring — for, every new Brother will go through the ceremonies of the three Degrees, which are basically, all about Ritual.

Some Brethren believe that our Ritual is not really for these modern times and should be minimized. Others, think that Ritual is the most important part of Freemasonry — and even stress, as the most important quality for progressing through the Line, that one has to memorize every word, even if we just repeat it by rote. It seems to this Mentor that these are the two extremes of the argument. And we prefer to situate ourselves somewhere in the middle.

We believe that Ritual has two very important components. First, it contains a large part of our Masonic teachings; it is a traditional tool to teach it and to have it penetrate in us, deeply. Secondly, Ritual is followed by Masons anywhere and everywhere, no matter which country or language, in quite a similar manner. This provides Unity and a sense of Communality.

This issue reminds me of my high school years. I was, at best, a C-average mathematics student until I found this wonderful teacher, Mrs. Ferrer. She said: "Jorge, you will never get mathematics, if you try to learn it by heart, as it were a poem, and then regurgitate it. You have to think it through". Then, she taught me how to derive all trigonometric functions and relations directly, from the graph of the circle with unit radius. After that, I became an "A" student, and have taught the topic for over forty years, at all levels.

It seems to me that the same occurs with Ritual. If we try to learn it by heart, as if it were a poem, and then to repeat it as a parrot, it will never make any sense, or provide any benefit, to anyone — including ourselves. But if we say it slowly, paying attention to all it conveys, to all its richness, even if we commit some memory errors, it will definitely do us a lot more good.

And only then, will we be able to convince our new Brothers of its importance, and have them learn it with gusto, too.

Fraternally/Jorge.

Jorge L. Romeu
Onondaga District Mentoring Chair

The Mentoring Corner

April 2016

Hello, Brothers!

In March, we gave two NorthStar presentations: one at our Liverpool Syracuse Lodge and another at Onondaga District MWD meeting. They raised much interest, questions and vibrant exchanges. Then, on March 16th, we gave a formal training to six Brothers. If need be, we are willing and able to present more training sessions. Let us know through our DDGM.

Summarizing, *NorthStar* is composed of two parts. *Candidate Selection* is where we learn if the prospect is a good match for our

Institution, and vice versa, saving much time and effort to both parties. Success Coaching is where the accepted candidate learns about the three Degrees and becomes an active member of his Lodge. Coaching accomplishes two very important issues: retention and integration of the new Brother, and *review* and *edification* of the course coaches.

Candidate Selection starts with the first phone or email contacts, and is followed by three personal interviews, where the prospect asks about Freemasonry, and coaches explain what we are not. It is here where those who seek a dining club, a place to conduct business or find new customers, discover that Freemasonry is not what they need. The prospect also learns about some history of Freemasonry, the Compact and our Landmarks (when was the last time we revisited them?). Prospect is also asked to respond to a questionnaire, and to write about himself.

The questionnaire and write-up are very important: they provide elements to discover the motivations and objectives of the prospect to join Freemasonry and to life in general. We explain that *Freemasonry is not just a one-time Event but a philosophy of life*, requiring dedication, time, resources, and an *open-ness* to new ideas that we then apply, to improve our daily lives.

We want the prospect to know our families, and for us, to know his. The Social Event is, thence, very important: bring his Lady to a dinner and meet the other Lodge Brethren. Without strong family support and understanding, a Brother will likely stop participating in Lodge ...

Finally, the last meeting is at the prospect's home. We show an LSOME video about our Institution. We explain how we have learned to know each other better and that, if the prospect so desires, he can request the Petition. The coaches now know him and can co-sign the form. A Lodge investigation provides additional material for his balloting. Once accepted, the Candidate follows Success Coaching, that helps him integrate faster and become an active Lodge member.

NorthStar also provides an opportunity for its Coaches to review and/or re-learn perhaps forgotten facts, via the readings and expositions given to the Prospect, and then to the Candidate.

Fraternally/Jorge.

Jorge L. Romeu
Onondaga District Mentoring Chair

The Mentoring Corner

May 2016

Hello, Brothers!

This month, I would like to bring up two topics: aspects of practical application of NorthStar and Lodge elections. They are intimately related.

Bro. Bob Bowles and your Mentor started implementing Candidate Selection with three new prospects for our Liverpool Syracuse Lodge. The first thing is that it implies a lot of work: we have to read and prepare for each meeting, duplicate the forms, write a short meeting report and read the material that the prospects return, in addition to answering their questions and giving them briefings about our Institution. But it is worth, every minute of it!

Our first prospect was scheduled twice and never showed up: an excellent result as it saved investing time and effort in someone who was really not very interested. Our second and third prospects are undergoing the NorthStar process. We have already had the first three, face-to-face meetings, and they have submitted their questionnaires and Introspection essays, and have asked many good questions about our Craft history, Landmarks, procedures, etc..

One issue that has come up with both of our prospects (and also among some in the 2016 class of AASR) is the interest in attending presentations and instructive activities in the Lodge. And this leads us directly into our elections that will take place this May. For, the possibility of having such activities, that inject much life into our Lodges, depends much on its Master.

Were this Mentor honored with this position in his Lodge, I would implement two things. First, I would take the Lodge into the First Degree, in every meeting, so that the newly raised Entered Apprentices and Fellow Crafts could attend at least part of the meetings. Sometimes we rush them through because we know they are in Limbo, until they have been raised.

The second thing I would do is to have a presentation or an instruction section in every meeting. There is much material available: our monthly *The Word* published excellent articles from yesteryears, Brethren can share books they have read from our GLNY Livingston Library or we can simply have a presentation. This Mentor has, in the past, already proposed that a Bank of Presentations be created. And that different Lodges could select one of them to be given.

A good presentation takes time and effort. Preparing one, to be given only once, is not a very efficient way to do things. But if we know that it may be given repeatedly, the effort will be greatly compensated with the joy of sharing ideas with our Brothers.

We now go dark for the Summer. Wish you all and your families a fruitful one!

Fraternally/Jorge.

Jorge L. Romeu
Onondaga District Mentoring Chair

The Mentoring Corner

August 2016

Hello, Brothers!

A dear Brother asked me a very interesting question during the recent St. John's Weekend, in Utica. "What are you up to", he said, "with all your work on Mentoring, and all the articles that you write for *The Word*? What are you pursuing? What is your agenda?"

This is a very legitimate question that maybe others may also have. So, I will answer it here, through a story about something that happened to me a few years ago.

At the time I was struggling with a presentation on Cuban Freemasons that I was going to give at the American Lodge of Research, in NYC. Watching me work, an intelligent, well-read and well-travelled young man (but not a Mason) asked me, point blank:

"Why do you dedicate so much time to Freemasonry, this unknown organization?"

I looked at him and thought: Should I be insulted? This young fellow respects me and has no reason to do so. Maybe Freemasonry is really unknown, to him and to his peers, in spite of all our efforts to make the Craft better recognized. Maybe we are not doing the right things...

Proclaiming that George Washington was a Mason, and that we support the MMRC in Utica, may sound too remote for them. Maybe, like in politics, the key issues *are all local*.

Perhaps, we should stress more our local activities such as Easter Egg Hunt, Halloween, Child ID, and Breakfast with Santa; our participation in food banks, our blood bank donations, or volunteering for children story-telling and school subject reviews, We can also organize our own activities, such as public presentations on interesting topics (e.g. hobbies, travels, history), given for the community at large. We can open and close Lodge, before and after the public function takes place in the Lodge social room, or in another appropriate area of the Masonic Temple.

We could also identify outstanding *XX Century Freemasons* in our own districts or state. We could draw up a list of such and sponsor a competition among Senior High School students. Then, we can give a $250 scholarship to the best Biography, and have a reading in the Lodge.

These are just some things that could be done to attract and keep community members in our Fraternity. Community activities that provide visibility to our Craft are also an important part of Mentoring! *The Craft makes some good men better, and the tree is known by its fruit!*

So, I answered back to my young friend: "Thank-you! You defined my agenda for the next 30 years: *to contribute in any way I can to make our Craft better known and more relevant*".

Jorge L. Romeu
Onondaga District Mentoring Chair

The Mentoring Corner
September 2016

Hello, Brothers!

Our *Editor's Prerogative* piece, in the September issue of *The Word*, mentions topics such as politics, its place in the Craft, and the power of Freemasonry to do right. Since we are in the midst of the Presidential Election season, this also seems a timely topic for *Mentoring*.

Independently of our political inclinations, we may probably agree that this campaign has been unusually bitter. The level of name-calling and caustic language used is far more than I have ever heard in my 36 years here. And we ask: what can Freemasonry do to help redress this situation?

Our Craft is well-known to foster *Brotherly Love and Tolerance*, which implies nurturing respect for others, and behaving as civilized human beings. If nothing else (and there is much more with our Craft) such contribution would be enough to justify the existence of our *Masonic Institution*.

When we are raised we are taught that our working tool is the Trowel, which we use in spreading *Brotherly Love and affection* — and not only within the walls of our Lodge! I like to think that one of our contemporary social problems is that there are not enough Masons out there to apply such important human quality, and promote it through our daily example, wherever our place in life is.

Half a Century ago, membership in American Lodges was more numerous than today. It spread over all occupations and professions, including in politics. To mention just a few, starting from World War II, we have Bros. Franklin Roosevelt, Democrat and

32nd President; Harry Truman, Grand Master of the Grand Lodge of Missouri, Democrat and 33rd President, and Gerald Ford, 38th President and a Republican. In the Senate, we have Bros. Strom Thurmond, Alan Simpson, Trent Lott and Robert Dole, all Republican; Sam Nunn and Robert Byrd were Democrats (Find 10,000 names and short bios of Freemasons in http://www.molorlibrary.org/10-000-famous-freemasons-4-volumes.html [link unavailable] or in http://freemasonry.bcy.ca/biography. They served in both political parties and included all ideological bents. These men argued and defended with passion, but with civility and respect, their principles and policies, and accomplished much work.

We contend that Freemasonry had a lot to do with such! It is difficult to call someone a Brother, in Lodge, one night and then, the following day, to insult him in the Senate floor, or in the press.

A second Craft contribution toward increasing civil relationships among politicians could have been *participation in Table Lodges*. For *men that share a meal together can work together*. Thus, leaving politics aside during dinner, Masons learn about and appreciate, their positive human and intellectual qualities. The resulting empathy helps them disagree without becoming disagreeable.

Such good features help attract more and better men to our Craft, and help retain them longer.

Jorge L. Romeu
Onondaga District Mentoring Chair

The Mentoring Corner
October 2016

Hello, Brothers!

MWGM Williamson has explained, in his St. John's Day speech, how our Grand Lodge will lose 20% more of its membership in the next four years. This is a serious matter, of concern for all masons, but especially for those of us who work in Mentoring. For, with a good Mentoring program, such loses may be reduced, and our Craft may be strengthened.

In search of information to better understand membership, I found two relevant articles by Bro. John Belton, the Editor of *Ars Quatuor Coronatorum (AQC)*, the research journal of the Grand Lodge of England (UGLE). They are *Masonic Membership Myths Debunked* (Heredom, V. 9, 2001, pp. 9-32), and *Does Rejuvenation Await Freemasonry*, (AQC, V. 121, 2008, pp. 163-183). They study the problem in the XX Century, in England, Australia, United States and New Zealand. They use yearly membership as well as raisings data, analyzed using the math model:

Membership-This-Year =

Members-Last-Year + Additions − Subtractions; where

Additions =

New-Raisings + Affiliations; and Subtractions =

Demits + NPDs + Deaths.

Bro. Belton shows several important results, including how Freemasonry reached a peak Before (and not After) WWII, relative to Total US Population (not to total membership). And how post war peaks were really due to an increase in raisings that started before WWII and Korea.

The analysis of Bro. Belton's math model also shows how: (1) increasing raisings alone will not, in the long run, increase membership (if poor retention). But (2) increasing the average length of the masonic life of our members, will! This, in turn, introduces two important factors: (3) good mentoring, to increase the retention of new brothers, and (4) recruiting them at a younger age, for older brothers will, due to biological reasons, have a shorter membership life.

MWGM Williamson also pointed out how slowing down our degree sequences could also help increase retention. A longer time between initiation and raisings allows more time (1) to provide additional masonic instruction and maturity to our new brothers, and (2) to foster a stronger interaction with other Lodge members, thus making the new brothers feel more at home.

Slower procedure may prevent new brothers from participating in Lodge, reducing their interest and triggering withdrawals. But this can be offset by lowering Lodge work to First or Second Degrees, allowing these new brothers to attend presentations, walk-throughs, instruction, etc..

Creating a **Bank of Presentations**, available to all District Lodges, may increase topic options. This Mentor has a presentation on the differences between York and Scottish rituals in Symbolic Lodges (First, Second, and Third Degrees of Masonry) that other Lodges can freely request.

Jorge L. Romeu
Onondaga District Mentoring Chair

The Mentoring Corner
November 2016

Hello, Brothers!

This month RW Bro. Jack Dombrowski and I taught a NorthStar workshop for a dozen Brothers at Liverpool Lodge. We need to train at least one Brother in each Lodge, to become its Mentoring Officer. And we need several more, to work in preparing new members.

There is a distinction between NorthStar's Candidate Selection (CS), and the traditional Lodge Investigative Committees, and Success Coaching (SC) Mentors and the MDC or LSOME.

NorthStar CS engages in a courting procedure: we want to know what is the interest and suitability of a potential candidate to become a Mason; we want the candidate know what we are and stand for, so he is not mislead. Some candidates learn about Masonry searching the Internet — not always the best source. So we need to correct some wrong concepts. We also need to identify their aspirations regarding our Craft — for we are not a business or political market, nor a dinner club. We explore their background and character — but we do not check anything. We just listen.

Lodge Investigative Committee takes our report plus that of *Guarding the West Gate* software, checks facts, interviews candidates, asks specific and pertinent questions and then evaluates them.

NorthStar SC works similarly to how the recent Onondaga Convention was developed: it explains and interprets the material in the different parts of the First, Second and Third Degree Rituals to the new Brother, in a one-to-one setting. MDC and LSOME courses, on the other hand, teach new Brothers using videos and texts. In addition, their instruction is given in groups.

Individual relationship between Mentor and Candidate is what characterizes NorthStar. It is also what requires that there be several Mentors in each Lodge, trained in NorthStar. Work is extensive and intensive; and a single Mentor will burn out trying to coach all the new Brothers.

One way to increase the number of Mentors is to pair one CS Trained, with one untrained Mentor, for each new Candidate. The untrained one would be the *apprentice*, and would become an independent CS Mentor after a full experience under the guidance of a Trained Mentor. The SC part of NorthStar is less complex; a seasoned Brother will perform after studying the Manual.

NorthStar purpose is (1) to recruit good men, and (2) to make good Masons of them at an early stage. But (3) to keep them among us, we also need to make Lodge sessions more attractive to them. It is necessary to do more than just pay the bills. This Mentor has suggested the creation of a *bank of presentations*, established in every District, for the use of any interested Lodge.

Last month we gave talk with its PPT, on the differences between the York and Scottish Rituals in Symbolic Lodges, at Seneca River Lodge. Anyone interested, just contact our DDGM.

Jorge L. Romeu
Onondaga District Mentoring Chair

The Mentoring Corner
December 2016

Hello, Brothers!

One of the main reasons for joining our Fraternity, that many of our Brethren have, is *Fellowship*. Especially in these days of Internet and cell phone communication, where many of our daily contacts are lacking a personal touch, the opportunity to get to know others with whom we may share values and ideas, and to develop friendships with them, is really a plus.

When we join a Lodge we get to know and befriend many new Brothers. But we can increase this experience by a simple expedient: *visitation*: the action of going to another Lodge and partaking in their work. As Masons, we have the right of visitation. When done properly, it is greatly appreciated by the visited Lodge, as well as greatly rewarding for the guests.

Visitation requires that (1) the caller is known (and vouched for) by at least one Brother, member of the Lodge; (2) the caller shows appropriate *documentation* (current Dues Card), or (3) undergoes an Examination (of Words, Grips, Signs) by the Lodge Senior Deacon.

We can always visit a Lodge on a personal level. But it is more fun to do so as an official event. In such case, the Master (or someone appointed by him, who will lead the visitation) can contact the Master or Secretary of said Lodge, to let them know of our forthcoming call and make the necessary arrangements. And here is where Mentoring of new Brethren is valuable.

First, new Brothers may not know of the *right of visitation*, or where, when, etc., another Lodge works. Then, it is only natural that new Brothers are shy to go on their own. It should be another function of Mentors to encourage and prepare such visits and accompany new Brothers.

In some countries, such as Britain, there are specialized Lodges for stamp collectors, gourmet cooks, or classic car fans. We don't have such lodges here. But, in New York City, there are Italian, German, and Hispanic Lodges that work in their own languages and have particular ways of implementing our Ritual. It is always interesting to watch and learn such new things.

We can also visit adjacent Masonic Districts. They are only a couple of hours drive away. We could organize some joint activities that enrich our experiences and strengthen our relations. And in the process, meet and befriend new Brothers. This would help in the merging process.

Grand Lodges in New York City and Philadelphia can be reached in a five-hour drive. Both have excellent museums and libraries, and beautiful lodge rooms. Trips to visit these Grand Lodges could also be organized, enjoying a tourism experience.

We take advantage of the Holiday Season to wish all Brethren and their families a fruitful 2017, with health, peace and brotherly love. And we thank God for all the benefits received.

Jorge L. Romeu
Onondaga District Mentoring Chair

2017

The Mentoring Corner

January 2017

Hello, Brethren!

Good Mentors need to be well read in Masonry. I have expressed, in our Official Visits, how NorthStar is as helpful for the new Brother, as it is for his Mentor! It provides strong motivation to seek more light in Masonry by every means at our reach; especially via readings.

For example, this issue of *Empire State Mason* brings an article by our Grand Lecturer, stating that the correct use of the plural of Brother is Brethren. Thence, I have corrected my article salutation. Also, *The Word* brings, in every issue, several interesting pieces that enrich our Masonic background. In the last few issues we read interesting articles written by Bro. Joseph F. Newton that have appeared in the Masonic newspaper *The Builder*, of the Grand Lodge of Iowa.

Lately, I have been reading an article by Bro. Albert Pike titled What Masonry Is and Its Objectives, delivered at the Grand Lodge of Louisiana in 1858. It is included in The Scottish Rite Ritual Monitor and Guide, by Ill. Arturo DeHoyos. It is particularly interesting to read how Bro. Pike describes the essence of our Fraternity. I am extracting below some important segments:

"To every Mason, *there is a God* — ONE, SUPREME, INFINITE in Goodness, Wisdom, Foresight, Justice and Benevolence .... To every Mason *the soul of Man is immortal*." (p. 54)

"At all times, *Humanity has had three chief enemies: the Despotism of Royal Power* ... the insolence, cruelty and bloodthirstiness of *The Sacerdotal Power* ... and the haughty pretension of *Rank, Caste and Privilege*, fenced about with exclusiveness" (p. 50)

"*Masonry* was made to be *The Order of the People*. It has ever exerted its influence on the side of civil and religious liberty; of emancipation of both the muscle and the mind of all that were fit to be free; of *education and enlightenment ... Devotion to the interests of the People, detestation of Tyranny; sacred regard for the Rights of Free Thought, Free Speech and Free Conscience; implacable hostility to Intolerance, Bigotry, Arrogance and Usurpation; respect and regard for labor which makes human nature noble; and scorn and contempt for all monopolies: that minister to insolent and pampered luxury.*" (p, 51)

"The Mason is devoted to the cause of *Liberty and Toleration, against Fanaticism and Persecution*, political and religious; to that of *Education, Instruction, and Enlightenment, against Error, Barbarism and Ignorance* .... And *Education, Instruction and Enlightenment* are the only certain means by which *Intolerance and Fanaticism can be rendered powerless*". (p. 45).

Read the entire paper in http://www.freemasons-freemasonry.com/pike_address_louisiana.html

Include, among your New Year Resolutions, means to increase your Masonic knowledge.

Jorge L. Romeu
Onondaga District Mentoring Chair

The Mentoring Corner

February 2017

Hello, Brethren!

Good Mentors need to be well-read in Masonry. At Initiation we are asked: what came you here to do? And we answer: to improve ourselves in Masonry. Here are two key issues.

First, grasp numerous **ways to learn more about our Craft**. Delivering the Ritual in a more deliberate manner will provide valuable information. For example, the answer to what induced you to become a Master Mason contains a profound lesson. Enumeration of all Lodge Officer's duties also provides important information. When we say, *to pay their wages, so no one leaves dissatisfied*, we can allude to many different and important things, both material and emotional.

The Word reproduces articles on different topics such as history, symbolism, or esoteric content, to satisfy its different readers. We can find one that we enjoy, and *discuss it in the Lodge session* — or at the gathering before the session starts. Some past Mentor articles include websites of interest that can be found in http://ecs.syr.edu/faculty/romeu/TheMentoringCorner.pdf

GLNY Chancellor Livingston Library has many interesting books and reading courses that can be found in http://nymasoniclibrary.org/. Any brother may request and read a book, then share his experience with his Lodge. Masonic Service Association's *Short Talk Bulletins* carries articles that can also be discussed in Lodge (http://www.msana.com/). Such discussion transforms passive activities into proactive ones fostering learning and member participation.

Second, individual activities require **the encouragement and support of a proactive Lodge leadership**. The Craft has a Leadership school: the Lodge Line. Aspiring Brethren are exposed to different positions in an increasing progression. When they acquire the necessary qualifications, they are moved up. But nothing says that Officers should be moved up automatically, every year.

Knowing the Ritual is only a part of being a Worshipful Master. Efficiency (doing things right) differs from effectiveness (doing the right things). The *Road to the East* and the *Master's Course* are two first-rate sources for aspiring Lodge Masters to learn from, and for Members to consider, at the time of electing new officers. Other important functions include preparing effective meetings, planning its topics and logistics, setting objectives, preparing and distributing the agenda. Conducting meetings requires listening skills, encouraging participation, handling overactive and over-quiet members, preventing petty controversies, reducing absenteeism, etc..

Worshipful Masters don't work alone, or in a vacuum. All Officers should be induced to participate. Work should be delegated, planned and shared by all, including *side-liners*. A good Officers Team can strengthen the Lodge, increasing attendance and membership by encouraging and supporting different Mentoring activities. Sometimes, we fail to remember these things.

Jorge L. Romeu
Onondaga District Mentoring Chair

The Mentoring Corner
March 2017

Hello, Brethren!

This year our Craft celebrates its 300th Anniversary. In 1717, four London Lodges gathered at the Goose and Gridiron Alehouse to create the first Grand Lodge. Freemasonry, as we know it today, was born (https://en.wikipedia.org/wiki/Premier_Grand_Lodge_of_England).

Sometimes, it is helpful to know where we come from, in order to assess where we are going to. I found in the Prestonian Lecture (http://www.masonicdictionary.com/prestonian.html) [page unavailable] titled *New Light on the Formation & Early years of the Gr. Lodge of England*, by Dr. Ric Berman, published in Vol. 129, 2016 of *Ars Quatuor Coronatorum*, very useful information.

Bro. Berman argues that a new concept of Freemasonry, with new characteristics, arose then, due mainly "to the changes brought about by new leadership, and not as the inevitable consequence of a continuing trend of measured evolution". He adds that "Freemasonry in the early eighteenth century was altered radically over a short period of little more than two decades to mirror the political and philosophical objective of those who led it".

Bro. Berman further states that "social organizations such as Freemasonry are a product of their environment ... that Freemasonry was adapted and molded – indeed, reinvented – in the second and third decades of the eighteenth century to fit new social and political parameters". There is much food for thought in the above assertions (the mentioned article is full of them).

First, we can recognize the importance that Leadership has in the direction of a Lodge: it can make or break it! Reading the article we learn how the old stonemasons guilds first admitted non-operative members (starting in the 1600s), who gathered *for social reasons*. Then, Brothers Anderson, Desaguliers, Payne and others, came into leading positions and *introduced Charges and Rituals, creating the speculative Freemasonry*, as we know it today.

Finally, we notice how *Freemasonry is a product of its environment*. For those of us who have practiced the Craft in other countries, such environmental (social and political) differences are a fact. For example, in the Spanish Caribbean (Cuba, Puerto Rico and Dominican Republic) the Craft has a stronger civic (non-partisan, but political) component. Having a less extensive democratic tradition, and fewer social organizations (Rotary, Kiwanis, VFW etc.), *Lodges have a more important role as organizations that engage in social and civil society issues*.

Such knowledge of the origins and the different characteristics of our Craft is also of importance to Mentoring. We are becoming a more diverse society. And as such, some of our new members may come from other countries, with different Masonic traditions. For example, this Mentor had to work hard at first to familiarize ourselves with the way the Craft worked here.

Jorge L. Romeu
Onondaga District Mentoring Chair

The Mentoring Corner

April 2017

Hello, Brethren!

On Saturday April 7th, we were having a Town Hall in Onondaga District, with DGM Charles Catapano. We were all looking forward to hearing his ideas about NorthStar Program. At the last minute, the meeting was canceled due to a conflict with another Masonic Event.

The issue is of importance, since we don't know how the new Grand Master will consider NorthStar program, which was created by our current Grand Master while he was DGM. Thence, NorthStar enjoyed four years of full support from above, that has allowed it to grow and expand.

NorthStar is not perfect. But we believe it has two very strong components. First, it gives the Candidate to our craft an opportunity to understand what we are about, and to assess if this is what they are really looking for. And it gives the Lodge an opportunity to assess the Candidate. This saves a lot of time and effort; Candidates that apply, tend to stay with us for a longer time. The second component is the opportunity to strengthen our own ranks: every Mentor needs to review or relearn his Masonic background, thus becoming a better informed Mason.

But NorthStar also has some implementation problems that need to be addressed.

With NorthStar it takes longer for a Candidate to Petition. Some may decide to drop the issue, altogether. It also takes time to form NorthStar Mentors, able to work with Candidates. As a result, the same Mentors may be reassigned to other Candidates — and Mentors may burn out. This may be solved by assigning more than one new Candidate to the same Mentor.

Some Candidates have no idea about Freemasonry — but others have relatives or friends, from whom they have learned about our Craft. In such cases, they may not need to spend several weeks with someone they do not know, assigned to instruct them. It might be more efficient to have their friends or relatives Mentor them, in an accelerated way, following NorthStar print.

Finally, there is the Protocol issue: how will the system of assigning Candidates operate in the Lodge? One alternative would be that the Brother receiving an interest message (e.g through the Web Page or the Secretary), passes it to the WM, who then contacts the Lodge Mentoring Officer. Considering whether it is totally new to the Craft, they either assigns a Mentor, or assigns the Brother that is introducing him to the Lodge, to instruct him. In the latter case, we provide this Brother with NorthStar Candidate Selection Manual and a short briefing.

We have seen lost opportunities because the Mentor or the WM of the Lodge do not know of someone's interest to join the Craft, until his Petition is read in Lodge by the Secretary. In this case, the advantages of running this Candidate through North-Star are likely lost.

Jorge L. Romeu
Onondaga District Mentoring Chair

The Mentoring Corner

May 2017

Hello, Brethren!

Every time I work on Mentoring issues, I remember a story I once heard about St. Francis of Assisi. He was a Catholic friar that lived in Italy during the Middle Ages. Francis was famous for his sermons and teachings. His life serves as inspiration for the hymn Prayer of St. Francis that goes: "Make me a channel of your peace; where there is hatred let me bring your love..."

The story goes that a young friar was assigned to the monastery where Francis lived. He arrived at dinner time, and Francis sat him at his side, and held some small talk with the novice. At the end of the meal, Francis said to him: "tomorrow at sunrise I will meet you at the main gate of the convent: we are going out together, to preach".

. The young fellow was so excited that he could not sleep that night. He was just imagining himself, standing next to Francis in the main square, surrounded by thousands of people listening to his marvelous sermon, so inspiring that, at the end, brought everyone to their knees!

The young friar was ready, by the main gate of the monastery, even before the sun came out. Francis appeared, and they went together out the door. Francis took out his rosary and started praying in a low voice. And the young priest did likewise.

They went up one cobbled street, and down another. They walked through the market. They crossed several large, and several simple *piazzas*. All the time, praying in low voice, with their rosary in hand, Finally, Francis stopped: they were again at the main gate of the Convent!

The young friar was startled. They had not stopped to lecture anywhere. They had not even uttered a word! He then timidly asked Francis: "I thought we were going to preach, today". Francis smiled and answered: "what do you think we have been doing all day long?"

As Freemasons, we all are Mentors. Not only to our new Brethren, but also, and perhaps even more important, to the community where we interact. Our position may be prominent, or it may be regular; our station in life may be a palace, or a street corner. That doesn't matter. What matters is what we do and say for others to perceive, that reveals our condition as Freemasons.

As in the story of Francis of Assisi, our performance within our environment will always be the best presentation about what our Institution stands for, and symbolizes. Be a good father and husband, a good neighbor and friend, a good worker and citizen, always sincere and helpful. People might comment: "what a nice person! And someone may reply: "He's a Freemason!"

Such is the best type of Mentoring that we can get; the best "advertisement" Freemasonry can have. Each one of us can become one such Mentor. It is all in our hands!

Jorge L. Romeu
Onondaga District Mentoring Chair

The Mentoring Corner

August 2017

Hello, Brethren!

On June 24th, Freemasonry arrived to its 300th anniversary. In 1717, four London lodges met to create the first Grand Lodge. Long before that, Masonic Lodges had existed, but operated independently of each other. The Grand Lodge provided Freemasonry with a structure, common rules, visitation rights and a modern philosophy. It was the beginnings of modern Civil Society.

In May, I contacted a dear Brother in NYC, and asked him what we were going to do about this. His answer was: "this is their anniversary, not ours". Respectfully and fraternally I made known my disagreement with such assessment. I strongly believe (1) this is an anniversary of our entire Fraternity, wherever it may exist, (2) celebrating such anniversary helps our Brethren to better understand our core beliefs, and (3) it enables our Institution to make itself better known by the general public. This constitutes, therefore, an important activity of our Mentoring function.

In 1717, nations were ruled by *hereditary kings*, whose *authority* was *derived* from God, and *individuals* were *judged by their hereditary rank* in a strongly *hierarchical society*. *Freemasonry* introduced several *revolutionary concepts*: men met "on the level" (*equality*), and were *assessed by their merits*, not their wealth or social status. Their *leaders* (lodge Masters) were *elected* by secret ballot. And their members had to respect (tolerance) the religious ideas of their Brethren.

What a set of revolutionary concepts, for their time and place! Such ideas, which were part of the movement known as Enlightenment, contributed to foster the French Revolution and its modern institutions! Freemasonry helped to bring them about, and to disseminate them around the world.

According to Prof. Margaret Jacobs (UCLA) the first Grand Lodges in Britain, France, and the Netherlands, were *Schools of Government*. According to Bro. Ric Berman (see The Word, March 2017) the first Grand Lodge, with its *Constitutions and Regulations, represented a Qualitative Change*. After several decades of evolution, the Craft became what it is today. According to our own research on Caribbean Freemasonry (in Cuba, Puerto Rico and Dominican Republic), the Craft was a *School of Leaders*. There, men interested in improving their society met, interacted and grew intellectually, at a time and place when few or no centers of higher learning, existed.

Freemasonry acquired specific characteristics from the societies where it flourished. Those who have visited lodges abroad, or even in different regions of the United States, have verified this. But its main ideas and beliefs remain the same. It is good to remember what these ideas were, how they came about, and how transcendental they were in their own time —and are still, today.

Knowing our history will make us better Masons. And making it known to the general public will help them appreciate the strong impact that Freemasonry had in Western civilization.

Jorge L. Romeu
Onondaga District Mentoring Chair

The Mentoring Corner

September 2017

Hello, Brethren!

As a Mentoring tool, our monthly *The Word*, is the best well-kept secret Freemasonry has in Central New York. This should not be so. We want to share here, some of its Mentoring uses.

Its primary use is to let us know what is going on: what has happened that we missed, or that we can congratulate our brothers for; or what will happen that is important, such as the District Conventions in October. Also, what programs will be presented in other Lodges, either to attend them, or to take notice thereof and replicate them in our own one. But that is just the beginning.

There is always *food for thought*, in the interesting articles that our Editor includes, taken from relevant publications of the past, such as *The Builder*. In addition to learning ourselves, we can use them for Lodge *instruction*. Lectures, where one Brother presents while all others passively listen, are not very productive. Also, not all presenters are engaging, not all material discussed is of interest to all. As a result, some Lodge presentations have very little effect — if any.

Finding good topics that interest most members and can be reviewed beforehand, to spark active discussion during its presentation is not an easy task. Where can we get enough copies for all? But we all receive *The Word* and the Lodge can select one of its articles. Members can choose one of them, and then bring the chosen article to discuss in Lodge. September issue's feature article was *Man and Mason*. Discussion topics include: Who was the article author? Who was Bro. Gould? What his main Masonic contribution? When and where was the first research lodge founded? Where can one find, on line, some of its stimulating research materials? (Hint: web site of the Grand Lodge of British Columbia and Yukon: http://freemasonry.bcy.ca/aqc/). [https://freemasonry.bcy.ca/index1.html]

In our *Editor's Prerogative*, we read an interesting and worth emulating Lodge activity. It says:

> "Another informative program we hope to book is a presentation on local drug abuse trends. We invited a Sheriff's Deputy to give the talk and we will open the doors to the interested public."

Our Craft needs to become engaged in the community where it resides. Its presence must be an active one, developing children, adults, families, special groups, and other activities that are open to all. Then, advertising to, and inviting the local community. If we want to attract new members, we must show them all the good things we do. By developing Lodge programs of narrow interest to us, and by keeping our activities to ourselves, we are not achieving this objective.

This year, our Craft celebrated its 300th Anniversary. Such important date should not pass by, unnoticed. One example of worthwhile activity would be an informative presentation, open to all the community, on the key principles of tolerance and responsibility that our Institution espouses!

Jorge L. Romeu
Onondaga District Mentoring Chair

The Mentoring Corner
October 2017

Hello, Brethren!

This Mentor has caught word about an incident that occurred in one of our Lodges. It seems that several of its Lodge members had a grievance against another one who had a relative that had petitioned to the Lodge. Such Candidate had been favorably vetted by the Lodge Investigation Committee. In the Lodge ballot, this Candidate was rejected by a few votes.

This is a Mentoring issue, as it deals with the rejection of a Candidate that the Lodge Committee assessed a worthy one. As a result, this Candidate was not initiated an Entered Apprentice and we lost a potentially good member. In addition, if the Candidate applies to another Lodge, he will be burdened with having to explain a previous rejection, which may have not been a result of the Candidate's own demerits, since the Investigating Committee did not find them.

This Mentor would like to suggest several more efficient ways to handle and resolve grievances, that may not interfere with the admission of Candidates into our beloved Fraternity.

If we have a grievance against another Lodge member, we can first raise it directly with this Brother. If this procedure does not produce results, we can discreetly bring it to the attention of one of the Lodge Line Members, or to the Worshipful Master, himself. These officers can then intervene and act as good faith intermediaries, to help resolve the issue at hand.

Furthermore, we can always, in open Lodge, bring up an issue before its members. The Lodge can then have an exhaustive discussion, where each side can present their case. The Lodge can then help find a fair and mutually satisfactory solution. Finally, there exists a Masonic Judicial System at Grand Lodge, with rules and regulations, where Masons can always submit their complaints.

This Mentor comes from a very hostile environment: Academia. There, bickering sometimes takes a very ugly face. We have heard horror stories about faculty voting against the Tenure of another faculty, who has previously voted down their own Promotion. Or about faculty that have failed a PhD student of another faculty, with whom they have had serious problems. Rest my case.

In another, more positive vein, as District Mentor I want to remind our Brethren that Grand Lodge sends all Candidate information received through their website, to our respective DDGMs. And these, in turn, send them to us, Mentoring Officers of each District, so these Candidates are assigned among the Lodges that develop the NorthStar program. If your Lodge is one of those who implements NorthStar, be sure to have your District Mentoring Officer know of it, so he can forward the Candidate information to you!

Finally, this is the epoch of District Conventions. They constitute a wonderful Masonic Experience: our Ritual knowledge greatly increases in them. And we get to meet many new Brothers from other District Lodges, enlarging our network. Find out when is your District Convention. And try to attend it!

Jorge L. Romeu
Onondaga District Mentoring Chair

The Mentoring Corner

November 2017

Hello, Brethren!

I just finished reading an article about animal husbandry. And I find many similarities between what they do to increase and improve their flocks, and what we do in our work as Mentors.

In animal husbandry, males and females are carefully selected, so that their offspring's health and strength will improve. Then, female are carefully managed during their pregnancy and delivery. The new born are vaccinated, and carefully managed during their first, tender months, to ensure they arrive to full adult age. Finally, to keep them safe and prevent they leave, good fences are built in their pastures.

As Mentors, we use the NorthStar Candidate Selection segment to help us discover good candidates, and prepare them to better receive their degrees. The Success Coaching segment of

NorthStar helps the newly raised brothers to fully understand and internalize the knowledge conveyed through images and legends included in our degree ceremonies. But we cannot build fences to keep these new brothers from leaving us. And we would like to find more ways to induce them to remain Freemasons for life.

One way to achieve this is through encouraging more participation in Lodge life. This can be done by presenting good, frequent programs. The November issue of *The Word* includes several articles that are not only excellent *food for thought*, but also excellent material to present or discuss in open Lodge. In addition, we can take advantage of the new Grand Lodge permission to open, close, and do Lodge work in any of our three degrees, to include these new members in such activities, from an early stage.

There is yet another way to retain new members in our Institution, and at the same time make our Lodges more visible and relevant in our communities. We could hold Career Days jointly with our DeMolay, and Triangle and Rainbow chapters. And then, open these programs to all youngsters in said communities.

Many of our own Brethren, such as this Mentor, are older, retired men with a long working life. We could share some of our working experiences with these young people, helping them take the tough decision of choosing their future road in life. We would gain four things. First, DeMolay is the quarry of our Craft; this strengthens it. Secondly, in this process, some of the other young attendees may become interested in joining DeMolay or Triangle. Third, the community will learn more about us, enhancing our visibility and perhaps also the interest of some good men joining the Craft. Finally, newly raised brethren can be invited to participate in such community activities, becoming part of such challenging projects.

This Mentor is willing and able to talk about industrial statistics, quality control, and on how to prepare students for a STEM (science, technology, engineering & math) college career. Interested DeMolay Dads or other Masonic youth group leaders are encouraged to contact us at our phone (315-476-8994).

Finally, we successfully had our District Convention. The new Rituals for opening and closing the Lodge in First and Second Degrees were rehearsed. And we were told that, even when not yet fully accepted, the First and Second Degree Rituals can already be used. They are really not very difficult to implement. If we know our Third Degree Ritual, the new changes are mostly predictable adjustments.

Jorge L. Romeu
Onondaga District Mentoring Chair

The Mentoring Corner

December 2017

Hello, Brethren!

In last month's *The Word*, we suggested developing a Career Day for DeMolay, Triangle and Rainbow, open to all youngsters and their parents. Onondaga District DDGM, RW Toth, has supported this idea. He put us in contact with Bro. Tom Perry of Morning Star Lodge, who runs DeMolay and is also an educator. Bro. Perry suggested conducting the event at Liverpool Lodge, which is centrally located and has three levels that we will use to meet, separately, with the youngsters and their parents. The Career Day will take place mid-February. We need volunteers to talk about their work experiences, job searches, financial aid sources, campus life, etc.. (Please refer to RW Toth's *The Word* article, for more information.)

We have had excellent input, so far. W. Russell agreed to facilitate Liverpool Lodge premises. Bro. Earl Tuttle suggested doing some "mock interviews". Another Brother suggested opening our Lodge room, for those interested in visiting it, and having a Brother there to answer questions and explain what objects, in the Lodge room, mean. Other suggestions include contacting local High Schools, getting brochures and a presenter from local colleges, and inviting the Eastern Star ladies to participate with us.

We will have both, male and female youngsters, so we want feminine role models and input. Therefore, we will invite Eastern Star ladies to provide mentoring, too. Then, we also want to work with youngsters' parents (as a grandfather and father, I learned that without constant prodding and aid, most kids won't be able to navigate, on their own, the complex applications, financial aid, and other paper required work).

The plan is that Bro. Perry announces the Career Day to our DeMolay and Triangle, and these invite their school friends and neighbors. Then, advertise the Career Day in local schools, and through the Neighbors supplement of the newspaper. We can work with the youngsters in one level of the Lodge: have speakers talk about their professions, trades, skills, etc., and conduct mock interviews and examples on how to write good letters of applications, on finding the corresponding references, searching for funding sources, etc..

In another level of the Lodge we would work with their parents, letting them know about the application process deadlines, how to help their siblings find financial support and sources of funding, find and apply for scholarships, etc.. We can invite someone from a College Admissions Department, or get brochures.

Some attending youngsters may become interested in joining DeMolay or Triangle. Perhaps some of their fathers may become interested in Freemasonry, and may visit our Lodge room (we can have a video about Freemasonry). Our Institution would become better known, and some visitors may even join our Craft.

Lodges should become more involved with their Communities. There was a time, when Masonic Lodges were strong pillars of their community. Becoming more involved and better known, as an Institution, will help attract good Candidates, and keep those we have attracted, as Masons for Life!

Finally, we pray to the GAOTU that 2018 brings all of us, and our families, health, happiness, and new challenges and opportunities to achieve success in our lives, and in our Lodges!

Jorge L. Romeu
Onondaga District Mentoring Chair

2018

The Mentoring Corner

January 2018

Hello, Brethren!

NorthStar Candidate Selection job is to help *discover good applicants* and prepare them to better receive their degrees. Success Coaching helps newly raised brothers to fully understand their degree ceremonies, and to induce them to remain Freemasons for life. Recruiting and keeping the new Brethren to our Craft, is both a Mentoring and a membership issue. Freemasonry, as well as several other social organizations, has experienced a severe decline in membership, during the past half-century.

Several studies have been undertaken to assess and off-set such decline. A recent one, sponsored by the Northern Masonic Jurisdiction of the Scottish Rite (AASR/NMJ), is reported in a recent Northern Light, the magazine of AASR/NMJ. It includes some results of such study, articles about Leadership in the Blue Lodge and a report on the Masonic Renewal Committee.

Established in 1988, the MRC is an incorporated body of the Conference of Grand Masters in North America. Its mission consists in developing innovative programs to reinvigorate the spirit of Freemasonry, within our Grand Lodges and its constituents Lodges. Its website is: http://www.freemasonnetwork.org/masonicrenewal2 [site unavailable].

This Mentor immediately explored the MRC web page. It contains an entire section of materials such as: http://static.smallworldlabs.com/scottishrite2/content/masonicrenewal2/PDFs/101Ways-to-improve-Interest.pdf [site unavailable], to aid Lodges in developing interesting The stated meetings; or to improve their Mentoring http://static.smallworldlabs.com/scottishrite2/content/masonicrenewal2/PDFs/Mentoring-for-Growth.pdf [site unavailable];

a PPT to help develop Lodges http://www.freemasonnetwork.org/masonicrenewal2/academic-lodges-program [site unavailable] on academic campuses, for faculty and students; and free and useful online Lodge workbooks and manuals http://www.freemasonnetwork.org/masonicrenewal2/lodge-development-workbooks) [site unavailable].

The **Freemasons Network** is a Forum and Discussion Group to share ideas and concerns, and to network with similarly-minded Brethren, that one can join for free. It is hosted by The Supreme Council, 33°, of the AASR/SMJ, in Washington D.C. MRC ran, only this year, the Bedwell Essay contest that sought new ideas about Masonic renewal from its members. The contest subject was "Concept of Masonic Renewal – What does it mean to you now, and in the future?" Essays were between 1000 and 1500 words. Monetary awards were given to the first ($1500), second ($1000) and third ($500) places. Essay submissions will be posted on the MRC website starting in March with the top prize winner. Then each month there will be a new essay posted until they run out, which will be in late 2021. These will surely provide a good read!

A seasoned colleague Educator of mine once received the visit of a very disgruntled parent of one of his students. "Sir, my son is not getting anything out of your class!" the parent stated. My colleague, with a gentle smile, and in low voice, replied: "I am sorry to hear that. You know, Education is like looking into a mirror: you get out of it just as much as you put in". The same can be said about Freemasonry.

To become better Masons and men, it is up to each one of us to follow up by reading the articles that we find in The Word, as well as in other materials, available through our Livingston Library.

Jorge L. Romeu
Onondaga District Mentoring Chair

The Mentoring Corner

February 2018

Hello, Brethren!

On February 17th we had, in Liverpool Syracuse Lodge, a District Sponsored Career Day for DeMolay, Triangle and Rainbow, also open to all High School students and their families. With this activity we expect to provide a service to our youth groups and our community, as well as to give The Craft some visibility and greater involvement. We are most willing to help any other district organize theirs, too.

In December, MWGM Williamson sent out an Edict making it mandatory for all new Lodge petitioners to include a West Gate background check with their documentation. The reasons for this are clear to us.

Many years ago, when we submitted our petition, our father and two uncles were lifelong masons. We had all lived in the same place for years. And everybody knew us well. Today, most inquiries we get are from individuals that seek us in the Internet. Most are as unknown to us, as we are unknown to them.

The way I handle this issue for the NorthStar program Candidate Selection (CS), is thus explaining to the petitioner:

> "When you join a Lodge all other members become your Brothers. And as such, you trust and deal, and even open your home to them. You need an assurance that all this can be done with confidence, and that you are not running a risk by befriending or inviting the wrong individual. And more important, perhaps, is such situation when you travel. Many of our Brethren, when they visit other communities for business, pleasure or family, they also visit the local Lodge. For, they want to have some fellowship and see how other Lodges do their work. But they also want to have an assurance that it can be done without risk. [Guarding the] West Gate, a background check, reassures us about our members. Thus, it is required from all".

Another issue that has arisen, during our CS activities, is that of the person's religion. We have processed several Christian (of all denominations), Jews and Muslim candidates. For those who are not Christians, we provide this material, taken from pages 37-40 of Brother Carl Claudy's "Introduction to Freemasonry".

Among other important things it says: "the Holy Bible is referred to as *the Great Light*. The practice may be, and it often is, different in other lands. What is vital and unchangeable, as a Landmark of the Order, is that a *Volume of the Sacred Law* be opened upon the masonic Altar, whenever the Lodge is open. Jewish Lodges may prefer to use the *Old Testament*; in Turkey, the *Koran* would be used; Brahmins would use the *Vedas*; if there are many different faiths, several holy books will be placed upon the altar".

An issue that we also discuss with tact with candidates is that of the *Letter of Introspection*. For, they will write about personal thoughts and issues. We have to establish the reason for it (e.g., candidates may want to let us know something about themselves, just as we have, during our CS meetings, let them know some things about us). Then, we must leave candidates leeway to include things they are comfortable with (not force candidates to discuss the entire list of topics in that section of the CS Manual). I suggest that they select topics they feel are relevant for us to better understand them, and their reasons to want to join us.

As soon as the weather improves, we plan to conduct another NorthStar workshop in Onondaga District.

Jorge L. Romeu
Onondaga District Mentoring Chair

The Mentoring Corner
March 2018

Hello, Brethren!

This month we want to comment on two issues: Career Day results, and the use of new technology to enhance Craft work. For, both affect Mentoring in an important way.

Our Career Day was a success: we demonstrated that it could be done, and developed a process that enabled us to assess its strong and weak points. We want to thank, for their participation, DDGMs Toth and Lort (who came from Alex Bay), WM Russell, Bros. Hansen, Rosa, Perry, Bertans and Busa, and Mr. Phil Grome from BOCES, and Mrs. Zoila Romeu from LaFayette HS.

Strong points included that our Lodge event was in the newspaper for two weeks; people visited, a team of speakers and a procedure to deliver the material, were established. Weak points include that no DeMolay, Triangle or Rainbow, or Eastern Star members attended the event. This is our fault, as our coordination efforts were not focused, and the lead time was short. Next year, when the Career Day is repeated, we will start planning earlier, and establish firmer contacts with all.

Another important issue is the use of technology in our work. Often, we need to hold meetings with Brethren that are away from each other, the weather is inclement, or there are scheduling problems. One way to successfully deal with this is through the use of "Telecons". These are phone conversations held between multiple callers, through a special number that allows all to listen and speak, as if they were in the same room. The service is free and easily obtained.

Suppose we want to hold a meeting in the height of winter, under severe weather, or that several meeting participants are out of town (say, enjoying sunny Florida). We can set up a Telecon at an agreed time. All participants can then call into said phone number and talk as if they were in a room. At the end, a list of phones and the total time they spent is sent to the Telecon "monitor".

Training is another example. This Mentor is preparing to run a NorthStar Webinar Training in April. We will hang a NorthStar Power Point presentation in the Web. Workshop attendees can watch the slides and call the Telecon phone, to listen to the explanations and ask questions. We plan three short sessions: (1) NorthStar need and generalities, (2) Candidate Selection, and (3) Success Coaching. Brethren interested in participating can register by email, giving their phone numbers so we can verify how they called in, and how they spent full time in the workshop.

Obtaining a Telecon account is free and simple. Go to https://www.freeconferencecall.com/ website and follow instructions. Lodges and Districts obtaining Telecon numbers will be able to pass along, to this new technology, some of their routine work, leaving personal interaction, always one of the most important and valuable features of our Craft, for more effective purposes.

Jorge L. Romeu
Onondaga District Mentoring Chair

The Mentoring Corner
April 2018

Hello, Brethren!

This month we want to comment on the *Lodge Line*; the mechanism our Craft has for training its leaders. For, indeed Lodge Leaders affect Mentoring in a very important way. And also, about the first Webinar for NorthStar training, that we will give this month.

We have seen in other organizations, and even in business and government, how some enthusiastic and well-intentioned individuals arrive to important leadership positions without the necessary knowledge of the organization and its operation to make it work efficiently. As a result they end up being a failure, in spite of all their good will and work.

In the Craft, future Lodge Masters first become Deacons and Wardens, which allow them to learn the Ritual, the floor work of the ceremonies and the different position requirements and obligations, among many useful things. When a Brother arrives to the Master's chair, he knows by practical experience, in addition to the formal training and manuals of the position.

But Leadership is more than just training and experience. It also requires some personal characteristics that are not acquired by habit. We have also seen in some organizations, and also in business and government, how very experienced individuals end up becoming terrible leaders. Thence, the risk of automatically moving up the Lodge Line, Brethren who may not yet be ready.

This Mentor is currently *Senior Warden* of his Lodge. And he may be elected Master, for next year. If granted this honor and responsibility by my Lodge Brothers, I would like to think it is because my Brothers feel that I that can do the job well — and not because it is "my turn".

Another issue of importance, this month, is the implementation of the first NorthStar Training "Webinar". This is an activity that we had announced last month, and that we will have on Wednesday, April 18th. We have "hanged" the NorthStar Power Point in our Web Page, and have provided our Telecon phone number and Access Code to all Onondaga District Lodges Secretaries and Masters, for them to pass on to interested Brethren. These can send me an email, with the phone number from which they plan to call. I can then identify them in the telephone callers' list of all callers to the event that I get as Administrator. This allows me to have a "roll call", and be able to give workshop attendees their participation Certificate.

If this first Webinar runs well, and we hope it does, we plan to conduct other Mentoring webinars in the future, for training and consultation issues. As the Telecon facility does not have a limit of callers, we may be able to extend an invitation to participate, to interested Mentoring Chairs of our neighboring Districts, served by *The Word*.

Jorge L. Romeu
Onondaga District Mentoring Chair

The Mentoring Corner

May 2018

Hello, Brethren!

THE MENTORING CORNER ~ 83

This month we want to talk about two sources of information, valuable and very useful for Mentoring work, and especially interesting for the newly elected Worshipful Masters.

The first source is the website for the Masonic Service Association of North America (MSANA.com). They mail their material to every Lodge and Grand Lodge Officer whose GL is a member of MSANA. Accordingly, most of our lodges should already be receiving them.

Short Talk Bulletins can be read in Lodge, or can be a source of a presentation. They are available in their web page. May's (http://www.msana.com/downloads/STB%20May%2018.pdf) [link unavailable] is about the Armed Forces Day. If a Lodge would prefer another topic, they can search the MSA Library section (http://www.msana.com/msalibrary.asp) [link unavailable] which contains a selection of items from the MSA web pages, and from previous items published or distributed by MSA.

The MSA Library includes interesting material at no charge. They include: the News Archive (http://www.msana.com/newsarchives.asp) [link unavailable], which contains past items of interest. The Audiovisual Archive (http://www.msana.com/audiovisual.asp) [link unavailable] which contains CD and videos created by MSA. Finally, Out-of-print MSA (http://www.msana.com/digitalpublications.asp) [link unavailable] publications and reports of bygone years, are also available.

The other source of information is http://www.masonicrenewal.org/about/ the Masonic Renewal website. The papers of the winners of the 2017 Essay Competition are now available in http://www.masonicrenewal.org/essays/ [page unavailable]. Their topic, "Masonic Renewal: What does it mean to you now and in the future?" can be used for inspiration, as well as for discussion in open Lodge.

The contest for the 2018 Bedwell Memorial Masonic Renewal Competition is now open: http://www.masonicrenewal.org/wp-content/uploads/2018/03/2018EssayContestRules.pdf [link unavailable]. This year's topic is "What is the Purpose of the Masonic Fraternity, now and in the Future?" Original work, 1000 to 1500 words, must be submitted by November 30, 2018. There is a money award.

Mentoring, in Freemasonry, like Quality, in an industrial organization, is everybody's job. Especially, of those elected as Lodge Officers. A good Mentor is a well-informed Mason.

We launched our first Webinar. As every new experiment, it could have been better. We plan to conduct monthly Mentoring webinars, starting in the Fall, for training and consultation. The Telecon facility does not have a limit for callers. We therefore invite all Mentoring Chairs of our neighboring Districts, to join, too. **Phone Number: 605-475-4831; Access Code: 710272**.

Jorge L. Romeu
Onondaga District Mentoring Chair

The Mentoring Corner

August 2018

Hello, Brethren!

Starting in September, I will be wearing two hats: Onondaga District Mentoring Chair, and Worshipful Master of Liverpool Syracuse Lodge. They will enhance each other.

THE MENTORING CORNER ~ 85

Let's talk Mentoring. In the past, candidates to the Craft came from family and friends of Lodge members. Today, some seek information on Freemasonry in the Web, or just talk about it. Then, they contact a Lodge or a Brother, and inquire about how to join our organization. Some of us, in our eagerness to bring new members sign Petitions for individuals we barely know.

Every First Line signer of a Petition for membership or Initiation should seriously reflect about his relationship and acquaintance with said Petitioner. What is the nature and length of his acquaintance with the Petitioner? Is the Petitioner a neighbor, a work colleague, a relative, a friend? Did you grow up together, lived across from each other, or worked, for several years?

Brothers must understand how serious it is to become the first-line signer of a Petition to our fraternity! When a Brother signs a Petition he is recommending that person. Every first-line signer is stating, on his honor, that he vouches for the integrity and worthiness of said applicant.

To sign a petition without knowing the individual is a risky procedure. To avoid this, the NorthStar Program was created. It takes the candidate down the road of Freemasonry, and learns more about him. And likewise, Candidates learn about the life-long commitment to our Craft.

If a Brother contacts a person interested in joining Freemasonry, but does not know him well, or long enough to recommend him, then *USE THE NORTHSTAR PROGRAM!*

The correct procedure is to pass the contact name and address to your Lodge NorthStar officer. From there, the NorthStar Program can be developed. After this program is completed, if you like, you can still sign said Petition jointly with the NorthStar Officer.

NorthStar places each candidate in the right level. It does not necessarily run all Program steps for everyone. Some candidates already have knowledge of Freemasonry, and can skip some NorthStar steps. Others know very little about us, and need to follow the entire sequence.

Finally, starting on September 4th, we plan to conduct a monthly Mentoring webinar, for training and consultation, every First Tuesday, at 7 PM. Our Telecon facility does not limit the number of callers. We therefore invite all Lodge and neighboring District Mentoring Chairs, to join us. The Telecon Information is: **Phone Number: 605-475-4831; Access Code: 710272.**

Jorge L. Romeu
Onondaga District Mentoring Chair

The Mentoring Corner

September 2018

Hello, Brethren!

We have received, as District Mentoring Chairs, a letter from RW.'. Joseph Passaretti, Membership Development Chairman of our Grand Lodge. His letter describes, in detail, the responsibilities of the NorthStar District Chairmen, in their important mission of Making New Masons (and not just new Members). The letter explains that our responsibilities include:

"To record all contact information of a potential candidate, who have been referred by the Grand Lodge or by any other source, into the NorthStar Portal and refer him to a lodge in your district, ensuring a good fit, for both, the candidate as well as the lodge; also informing the master of the Lodge and the CSO/Success Coach who has been assigned, by the master, to the potential candidate. We also would like you to explain the NorthStar Portal login procedure to each of the CSO/Success Coach in your district. The CSO/Success Coach will then continue to update the information on that potential candidate as he advances throughout the Northstar Process. If a potential candidate contacts the lodge directly, the lodge CSO/Success Coach, who the master has assigned, should enter the contact information into the NorthStar Portal."

In this article we summarize said information, for each Lodge CSO/Success Coach chair (which means that each Lodge **Must** appoint one!). And we will propose to our DDGM that, in our forthcoming MWD meetings, we take some time to go into further details. The alternative would be to conduct a Webinar, for all Lodge CSO/Success Coach chairs.

However, our past experience with Webinars has not been good. On September 4th, at 7 PM, we conducted the monthly Mentoring webinar for NorthStar training and consultation that we announced in our past *The Word* column. Nobody attended it. They will be discontinued.

In general, to access your CSO/Success Coach Lodge account, first go to the Grand Lodge website (nymasons.org). Notice how,

on the lower right side of this site main page, there is a NorthStar icon. Click on this icon and move to said web page. You will have received by mail a transitory password. Use it to gain access, and then change it to something you easily remember. If you have problems or questions, contact RW Passaretti: [email redacted]
Note how, CSO/Success Coaches in each lodge will only have access to their own lodge account, for entering potential candidates. The NorthStar District Chairman, in turn, will have complete access to all NorthStar accounts, from all Lodges in the entire District.

If a NorthStar Mentor acquires a Candidate in his Lodge, he processes it directly into his website. In turn, if a District Chairman receives a candidate from GLNY, he will refer it to one of the Lodges in his District, ensuring a good fit, for both, the candidate as well as said lodge.

Jorge L. Romeu
Onondaga District Mentoring Chair

The Mentoring Corner

October 2018

Hello, Brethren!

We all need mentoring at some point — and not only newly inducted brothers. I was going to write about two excellent opportunities: the NETFLIX series *Inside the Freemasons* (about the [United] Grand Lodge of England), and the international conference "Freemasons in the Transatlantic World", that took place at the George Washington Memorial, in DC, September 14 to 16 past.

Instead, I will write about an excellent article published in *The Builders*, in 1919, and reproduced in *The Word* last month, about which our Editor fittingly asked: "has it applications today"? It was not written by John Doe; but by the Grand Master of the Grand Lodge of Iowa.

I believe it is very timely, and would provide an excellent vehicle for a lively discussion in our Lodges. I will simply quote some of its content, leaving the reader to judge, by himself.

> "[Returning WWI soldiers] will find some institution which is lagging behind the times, failing to live up to its possibilities. ... They will discard it and build a new one, ... or they will step into the places of leadership, and force it to become *efficient*".
>
> "Their first question ... will not be *what have you done?* but *what can you do?* They will not listen to platitudes. ... They will not be satisfied with mere growth".
>
> "What are your *principles*? ... What will you do to make those principles *effective*?"
>
> "Great numbers of new recruits have swamped us with ritualistic work, making necessary the drafting of every officer for that alone, ... consecrating ourselves to mere mechanical memorizing of a ritual, ... preaching principles, living too much in a dead past, and wasting our opportunity to become a vital force, working as an institution for the good of mankind."

"Masonry is a living force, and not a dead fossil. ... Apply our age-old principles to modern conditions, interpreting the educational ideals of our Second Degree in terms of our twentieth century life, ... we have not been the active, positive force in the world."

"The activities of the lodge ... take too little account of civic duty, to which we are pledged in our obligations. ... The world credits us with a far greater influence than we really possess. ... The real challenge to us is that we prove the worth of that fraternity".

"The cry of the hour in the nation is for leadership. ... Masonry has a contribution of infinite value to make to America".

As a Mason, and as an immigrant myself, I am powerfully moved by this article.

Jorge L. Romeu
Onondaga District Mentoring Chair.

The Mentoring Corner

November 2018

Hello, Brethren!

Today, I want to share three excellent learning opportunities that I found recently. They enhance our knowledge of history of the Craft, and can also be used for discussion in Lodge.

The first is the NETFLIX series *Inside the Freemasons*, a production of the BBC and the Grand Lodge of England that consists of five, 45 minutes, episodes. Each one is associated with a theme: a look at the origins of our Craft, in England; overview of the ceremonies of Initiation, Passing and Raising (without giving away any secrets); some new activities that modern (young) English Freemasons develop in their Lodges, interviews with different members, etc..

Some of us have had an opportunity to see how Lodges work in other countries (or other US states). The practice of Freemasonry may vary in different places, and it is interesting to see how this happens. This series may be especially appealing for those Brethren who have not had such an experience. It may help enhance our outlook of Freemasonry throughout the world.

The second, an article published in the Washington Post, is about history of Freemasons in New York State. It includes a summary of the Morgan Affair, and the ensuing Anti Masonic movement of the 1800s. These two events practically shut down the majority of New York state Lodges, for twenty years. See: http://www.watertowndailytimes.com/national/skull-identified-as-anti-freemason-candidates-20181022

The third, is the AQC international conference Freemasons in the Transatlantic World, that took place at the George Washington Memorial, in DC, on September 14 to 16 past. It was organized by Quatuor Coronati, the oldest research lodge, in London, UK. The three days of presentations, by well-known Masonic researchers, included a debate on the formation of the first Grand Lodge, a demonstration 'Universal Lodge' meeting, and tours of the Memorial. Registration was $115, and included frugal breakfast and lunches. A summary can be found in: https://scottishritenmj.org/blog/an-abstract-from-freemasons-in-the-transatlantic-world, and the program:

http://themagpiemason.blogspot.com/2018/02/freemasons-in-transatlantic-world.html

Finally, I am writing on Mid-Term election day. The current tone of public discourse is deplorable, as it encourages division among us. The fine art of disagreeing, without becoming disagreeable, seems to have disappeared. Playing the blame game will not help to find a solution.

Freemasonry, one of the oldest organizations of civil society, can play role to help diffuse this anger. *Our Craft is the Institution of brotherly love, harmony, tolerance and fellowship.* And the current hostility among Americans provides us with an opportunity to serve our country.

We must find ways to provide examples of harmonious and respectful problem resolution behavior, and encourage their use in the public arena. Such activity would help attract attention to our organization, and increase the interest for, and perhaps the desire to, join the Craft.

Such activity, thence, constitutes an effective and valuable form of Mentoring.

Jorge L. Romeu
Onondaga District Mentoring Chair

The Mentoring Corner
December 2018

Hello, Brethren!

Onondaga DDGM, RW Bro. Dombrowski, shared some information regarding Mentoring that circulated at a recent Utica membership workshop. It dealt with how to promote The Craft and best portray our Lodges through publicizing, and targeting our audiences. Examples can be found in discovermasonry.com and in eldon.nyc/nymasons.com [site unavailable] websites. I have gone through some of this information, and would like to reflect about its contents and implications.

Grand Lodge of NY website Discovermasonry.com has valuable information and photos describing who and what we are, and provides interested individuals, the steps to take to join us. It is well done and usefull, especially to counter much inaccurate or unfriendly information other sites carry. Site www.eldon.nyc [site unavailable] belongs to an advertising organization, and provides tips about how to best market our brand to the public at large. As an *old school guy* I find *commercial* Ads unfitting for the Craft. The website includes tips on how to create attractive web pages. However, sometime it is more effective to have *a simple but up-to-date site* that most Brothers can handle.

Attracting applicants is only half the battle. The *most important* and labor-intensive part is to *keep them among us*, and to *grow them into good members*. That activity is *Mentoring*.

Some *relevant aspects* include *making them feel at home* among us. Assign a Mentor to each new Brother: to sit with him, introduce him to other Lodge members, answer his questions, listen to his comments and complaints, encourage him to join the Line or Lodge Committee, etc..

Provide Light: explain (not re-read) the wealth of information in the Degree Rituals, give them (or suggest) books to read, or courses to take. If the new Brother is a reader, the Chancellor Livingston Library is appropriate. If he is not, the *Short Talk Bulletins* may be a better option.

Provide efficient Lodge time: every *meeting* has to be *informative, useful and pleasant.* This is easier said than done. Now that I am also Master of my Lodge, I can see how demanding this can be! Every member, individually and at Committee level has to contribute, to achieve it. The Master cannot, by himself, put all the necessary ingredients of a good meeting together. He is like an orchestra director: provides overall direction. Every brother has to play his part. To have good meetings will be more efficient to keep members, than any website or ad campaign.

Lodges can learn from each other, and help each other in said tasks. I miss terribly our MWD meetings. There, we shared our good experiences (to replicate) and bad ones (to avoid). And *fellowship among Officers*, from different but neighboring Lodges *encourage visitations.*

Mentoring reminds me of the subject of *quality* (a topic that I teach in engineering). Some managers say that Quality (or Mentoring) is job number one! But employees say: it is Quality Control's Department job. Both are wrong: *Quality (and Mentoring) is everyone's job!*

I just gave another NorthStar training workshop. Brethren from several districts attended. It was a pleasure to share. I am sure these Brothers will now be much *more efficient Mentors.*

Jorge L. Romeu
Onondaga District Mentoring Chair

2019

The Mentoring Corner

January 2019

Hello, Brethren!

I have been considering issues that move people to join (or not) our Craft, outlining our most valued and valuable commodities. Is it wealth? If we lose a dollar we can earn, borrow or find another one. Is it knowledge? Millions of people have very little of it, and still live properly. Is it time? Yes! For, if we waste one minute, we will never recuperate it! We will live one minute less, of our life. Cautious people value their time highly, and invest it wisely. Sensible societies invest their members' time judiciously, so they feel they are getting the most out of it.

How, then, can we better invest our members' time, so they are contented? We must first identify what their interests are. Fulfilling them is where our greater satisfaction is derived.

Different people have different interests. In my years in the Craft I have found four issues that most Brethren prefer: fellowship, esoteric, improvement, and service. Let's talk about them.

In a recent TV program I learned how *loneliness* damages one's health more than high blood pressure, alcohol abuse, or tobacco. As one ages, one retires, loses his companion, empties his nest, etc., and one becomes lonely. We find couples eating in restaurants, texting instead of talking to each other. One can thus be lonely, in the midst of the crowd. Lodge Fellowship can help mitigate our loneliness by providing trusted brothers with whom to share, and to confide.

Other Brothers enjoy studying esoteric subjects or partaking in rigorous ritual work. We have Research and Observant Masonry Lodges, where they will find such activities. All Lodge officers might also profit by visiting them, at least once every year, to improve our ritual work.

We say: *we came here to improve ourselves in Masonry*. But, what is precisely Masonry? To me, it includes everything that is good and beneficial to our lives. Our Craft teaches through allegories; we don't have to take everything literally. In ancient times, geometry was state of the art. These days, it may prove more useful to learn how computers, the Internet, software, etc., can help us. There is no reason why we cannot establish interest groups, where Brothers can teach each other these abilities, which will benefit their careers. UGLE [United Grand Lodge of England] organizes such Lodges.

Then, there are Brothers that want to work on behalf of society at large. Lodges used to be important community pillars. We don't need to put another man on the Moon, but we can well discuss the current drug problem. Our Masonic Compact states:

leadership is best demonstrated by commitment to serving others. These others may well be members of our village, town, state, or even our country. We don't want to (nor should) go into partisan politics. But we can well talk about important issues that affect our immediate or broader communities. Brothers interested in applying specific solutions to said problems can then join, outside the Lodge, to implement them.

Finally, in every Lodge meeting we should include a segment to make our Brothers think critically. *The Word*, which we all receive, published the article *What a Master Mason Ought to Know*. I plan to ask Liverpool Lodge Brethren to read it, to discuss it in a forthcoming meeting.

Jorge L. Romeu
Onondaga District Mentoring Chair.

The Mentoring Corner

February 2019

Hello, Brethren!

It is difficult to figure out where we are heading, if we don't know where we are coming from. So, I would like to talk about the beginnings of modern Freemasonry, which is usually considered at the creation of the Grand Lodge of London and Westminster, on June 24, 1717.

As usually upheld (https://en.wikipedia.org/wiki/Premier_Grand_Lodge_of_England), "four existing Lodges gathered at the Goose and Gridiron Ale-house, in London, and constituted themselves a Grand Lodge. These four lodges had previously met together in 1716, at the Apple-Tree Tavern", to start planning the formal creation of a Grand Lodge. Since the mid 1600s, some masonic Lodges, in England and Scotland, included Accepted Masons. Lodges remained separate, and each Lodge had particular rules. A Grand Lodge would create a unified and orderly society.

Last year Prescott and Sommers, two academic researchers, presented a paper (*Searching for the Apple Tree*) refuting this date. They instead proposed 1721, when the Duke of Montagu was elected Grand Master, as the true date of creation of the first Grand Lodge. They claim that there is no corroboration of a 1717 meeting, either in the daily press, nor factual documentation.

They claim that it was not until 1728 and later, in Grand Lodge minutes and Anderson's Constitutions, that the 1717 events were first mentioned. On the other hand, the 1721 election of Duke Montagu, was in the London press. In addition, they found several other inconsistencies.

Quatour Coronati Lodge of Masonic researchers (QC) disputed this, arguing that 1717 was just an initial date. Moreover, that Anderson, Desaguliers, Payne and Delafaye, Masons behind this initial endeavor, were not prominent figures of London's society -but that they were looking for one, such as the Duke, to head Grand Lodge and give it distinction. It took several years to achieve it. QC contends 1717 is the start of an important organization that peaked with the 1721 election of Duke Montagu, to head the Grand Lodge and make it well-known to society.

QC research argues that Grand Lodge organizers were supporters of the new Hanoverian dynasty: protestant, established in 1715, and considered illegitimate by descendants of a former, deposed, pro-catholic king, residing in France. Thence, according to contemporary political events, 1717 is a more a realistic date in which to create such new group to support Hanoverians.

The important thing is that modern Freemasonry, an organization that fosters *tolerance*; that encourages free and well-informed *thinking*; that assesses men according to their *merit*, and not their wealth or social status; that is governed by *elected*, instead of hereditary leaders, was created. These were, at the time, *revolutionary* ideas, in a world dominated by kings and nobles, and teared apart by religious wars — ideas that are still very unique. In our opinion, whether the first Grand Lodge was created in 1717 or 1721 is an academic exercise. Exact date is irrelevant.

Finally, we have given here some names, with the intention that the interested reader may look them up in Google, or other sources. This Mentor is not in the business of self-importance.

Jorge L. Romeu
Onondaga District Mentoring Chair.

The Mentoring Corner

March 2019

Hello, Brethren!

The question *What did we come here to do?* was asked from us during *our Initiation*. The two part answer included: *to improve ourselves in Masonry*. Below, we provide some useful and freely accessible Masonic websites. They contain a wealth of information that help increase our knowledge about the Craft. Reading is part of our self-mentoring process.

GLNY Livingston Library: https://nymasoniclibrary.org/

Onondaga & Oswego Mas. District Historical Society: http://www.omdhs.syracusemasons.com/

Masonic Renewal Committee (MRC): http://www.masonicrenewal.org/about/

Masonic Service Association (MSA) [of North America]: http://www.msana.com/

GL of PA Education System: http://education.pagrandlodge.org/

GL of PA Online Mentoring: https://pagrandlodge.org/online-mentoring/

GL of PA Library Catalog: http://1150.sydneyplus.com/MasonicLibrary_SE_Final/portal.aspx

GL Iowa Library System: https://grandlodgeofiowa.org/library-2/#/77/1750 [link unavailable]

GL British Columbia (GLBC) History of Freemasonry: http://freemasonry.bcy.ca/history/index.html

Duncan Masonic Monitor: http://www.sacred-texts.com/mas/dun/

MacCoy Masonic Books: http://www.macoy.com/Search.aspx?k=short%20talks [link unavailable]

Masonic Dictionary of History: http://www.masonicdictionary.com/history.html [site unavailable]

Famous Freemasons: http://www.masonicinfo.com/famous.htm

Scottish Rite Journal (SMJ): https://scottishrite.org/media-publications/scottish-rite-journal/past-issues/

Scottish Rite Museum and Library (NMJ): https://www.srmml.org/library-archives/

Some sites contain interesting articles on history (e.g. GLGB); others provide online courses; others contain catalogues of extensive masonic libraries (e.g. Libraries of GL of Iowa, PA and NY); others have Museums that we can visit online (e.g. AASR NMJ & SMJ); others contain ideas for Lodge meetings; (e.g. MSA, MRC); others have Degree work (Duncan).

We can read them individually, or we can discuss them, as part of our Lodge Education Programs. Remember: a Knowledgeable Mason is a Good Mason (or vice-versa).

Jorge L. Romeu
Onondaga District Mentoring Chair.

The Mentoring Corner
April 2019

Hello, Brethren!

By the time this column appears in *The Word*, we will be preparing to attend out Grand Lodge annual meeting. It is useful to review some basic history about American Freemasonry, in its first years, and about the organization of the Grand Lodge of New York.

According to https://en.wikipedia.org/wiki/Grand_Lodge_of_New_York#History it is not known when the first Freemason set foot in the colony of New York. The first documented event dates from the mid-1730s (and remember that the Grand Lodge of London was created in 1717).

In the 1750s the Grand Lodge of England split into two rival Grand Lodges: Antients and Moderns, who started chartering Lodges in North America under their own jurisdictions. Antients

New York Lodges retained their charter throughout the American Revolution. Thus, it was under this charter that an independent "Grand Lodge of Free and Accepted Masons of the State of New York" was created in June of 1787, with Bro. Robert R. Livingston as its first Grand Master.

St. John's Lodge, chartered in 1757, is the oldest operating Lodge under the jurisdiction of the Grand Lodge of New York. It is the custodian of the "George Washington" Bible, as it was upon such Bible that George Washington took his oath of office as our First President.

Grand Lodges (https://en.wikipedia.org/wiki/Freemasonry) are independent, sovereign bodies that govern Masonry in a given country, state, or geographical area (called a *jurisdiction*). *Exclusive* Jurisdiction is a concept whereby only one Grand Lodge will be recognized in any geographical area. If two Grand Lodges claim jurisdiction over the same area, all other Grand Lodges will have to choose between them. In 1849, for example, the Grand Lodge of New York split into two rival factions. Each claimed to be the legitimate one. They eventually re-united. Today, when our Grand Master is elected from Up-State, our Deputy Grand Master is elected from Down-State, and vice versa. In many European countries, such principle is not followed.

In Europe, things were somewhat different. English Freemasonry spread to France in the 1720s, first as Lodges of expatriates and exiled *Jacobites*. And then as distinctively French Lodges which still follow the ritual of the *Moderns*. During the 18th century, Freemasonry spread from France and England to most of Continental Europe. And from there, it spread to Latin America and the rest of the world which, at that time, was largely colonized by the European powers.

The term Continental Freemasonry was used in Albert Mackey's 1873 "Encyclopedia of Freemasonry" to "designate the Lodges on the Continent of Europe, which retain many usages which have either been abandoned by, or never were observed in, the Lodges of England, Ireland, and Scotland, as well as in the United States of America". The so called Continental Freemasonry is, in general, fairly different from American Freemasonry. And some of its Grand Lodges or Orients are not recognized by American Grand Lodges.

It is good to know where we come from. For, *a Knowledgeable Mason is a Good Mason.*

Jorge L. Romeu
Onondaga District Mentoring Chair

The Mentoring Corner

May 2019

Hello, Brethren!

Last month, our Editor published an excellent article about the Fellowcraft experience, taken from the February 1919 issue of *The Builder*. It was written by Bro. Haywood, and its title is *Part IV, the Middle Chamber in Speculative Masonry*. Our Editor had also published, in the March issue, the preceding article of such series, titled *Fist Steps, about the Entered Apprentice experience*. In it, we heard about the book "Lectures on the Philosophy of Freemasonry", by Bro. Roscoe Pound, Dean of Harvard and past Deputy Grand Master of the GL of Massachusetts.

Said book (not easy to read) discusses the life and works of four Masonic philosophers: Preston, Krause, Oliver and Pike. Bro.

Pound examined how these four answered *three key questions about Freemasonry*: (1) What is the *nature and purpose* of Freemasonry? (2) What is (and should be) the *relation* of Masonry *to other institutions*? (3) What are the *fundamental principles* by which Freemasonry is governed, considering the end it seeks?

The first of these four authors, Bro. William Preston, interests us today. For, Bro. Preston wrote the Middle Chamber lecture, as well as all the others in our degree rituals.

Bro. Preston was born in Scotland, in 1742, the son of a well-educated, minor legal clerk. He was orphaned at an early age, and was apprenticed to a printer, where he learned his life-long trade. As a young man, Bro. Preston moved to London and became a printer in the King's press. There he had the opportunity to proof-read and set into print, many of the most important books and articles of his time. This experience helped him acquire an extraordinary education.

Bro. Preston joined Freemasonry in his twenties, and soon became Master of his Lodge. He then made a point of learning as much as he could about the Craft. At the time there were few rituals. Degrees were conferred by reading the Old Charges to the initiates, and then commenting on their main content. Bro. Preston started writing his lectures, which later became the rituals we know today. He organized a sort of club of well-rounded Brethren, that would meet weekly to read and critique his lectures. In 1774 a system of rituals was complete and sanctioned by Grand Lodge, who adopted them in their Lodges. Bro. Preston taught his lectures in a Masonic society. Through them, they came to America, where they are the foundation of our Craft lectures, today.

Bro. Preston thought of Masonry *as a school*, where Brethren would obtain knowledge. Thus, *the Middle Chamber constitutes a synthesis of the main topics of his time*. Bro. Pound, and others, advocate *modernizing these topics to themes of our own times*, keeping the essence which is to instill in our Brethren *the importance of educating one-self and of advancing in life*.

For example, in the Spanish Antilles, during the XIX Century, there were few institutions of higher education. And Lodges were the place where men would acquire knowledge, practiced and honed their reading, writing and speaking skills, and made contact among them. Many of the most important leaders of such period learned and improved themselves in their Masonic Lodges.

Jorge L. Romeu
Onondaga District Mentoring Chair.

The Mentoring Corner

August 2019

Hello, Brethren!

Everybody needs a Mentor, sometimes. I have one: a Mason of 30+ years that has served in all Grand Lodge positions. Like I do every summer, I went to visit him, told him that I had completed my year as WM, and asked him where he thought I should put my future efforts. His answer was immediate: "In Education, Jorge. We need Masonic Education!"

So, I will continue as District Mentoring Chair, as long as our DDGM wants me to. And I will continue writing a monthly article for *The Word*, as long as Editor RW Zabriskie allows me.

I will then review the District Chair NorthStar procedures, as this is especially important for the new Lodge Masters and Secretaries. All starts when I receive an email from RW Passeretti with the names, addresses, phones and emails of individuals that accessed our Grand Lodge website, inquiring about joining Freemasonry. I then assess if there are Lodges close to said Candidates' residences, and if there are NorthStar trained Brothers in the selected Lodges, that can help them.

I then send an email to the WM and Secretary of the selected Lodges, with the information about the prospective candidates. I ask them if they are willing to process them. At this time, they don't need WestGate investigations; just to undergo the NorthStar process.

I do need a yes or no reply, from the Lodges, in short time, as I have to respond to RW Passeretti about their status. If a Lodge says they won't, I will then select another Lodge. A failure to give timely reply will unnecessarily delay starting the NorthStar process. We have an obligation to provide an answer to potential Candidates, in a reasonably short time, for Grand Lodge will ask me about their status. If the Lodges agree to process the Candidates, I send them an email, cc/d to said Lodges WMs, informing them that they will shortly be contacted by said Lodge Master.

NorthStar is not mandatory. It can be tailored to the Lodge or Candidate needs or wants. But it is helpful to implement even an abridged form. I would recommend, at the very least, to have one face-to-face meeting, explaining the Candidates what we are and stand for, and asking them why they want to join us. I would also invite them, and their significant other, to attend a Lodge open function. Other Brethren can then meet the Candidates, and they can meet several Brethren. It is a good way to assess if Candidates will be a good match for the Lodge, and vice versa.

Only then, I would offer Candidates an opportunity to request a Petition. By then, we all have an idea of what we are getting into. This approach reduces attrition and helps make better Masons. If questions, contact me by email, or ask me during our DDGM Official Visit to your Lodge.

Jorge L. Romeu
Onondaga District Mentoring Chair

The Mentoring Corner

September 2019

Hello, Brethren!

As a lifelong Educator I have struggled (and so, most of my colleagues) to define the meaning of "Education", as each teacher understands it in their own way. Something similar occurs with our Masonic Education I would suggest two things. First, paraphrasing our First Degree Ritual (see p. 46): "direct your [education efforts] by the Light you shall find, and as you may find it". Then, find adequate material, especially those that we can all access, and thence discuss it in Lodge.

I will suggest three reading soures that we all have, or periodically receive: the "Standard Work and Lectures"; the *Empire State Mason* magazine; and *The Word*. We can select readings and then, in open Lodge, discuss and explain them, especially to the recently raised Brethren.

From the *Standard Work*, constantly re-read the Opening and Closing sections, and also Degree work: especially the contents of Obligations and Charges. We should always keep these in mind.

The *Empire State Mason* always brings two or three interesting articles. In the Summer issue, for example, our Deputy Grand Master writes about Moving Toward Light (p. 8):

> "We should carry lessons learned into practice"; "be proactive; live according to our teaching", etc..

The Grand Senior Warden writes (p. 9):

> "What is more important: the ritual and Degree work, or having programs in our meetings? ... Lodge should take time to evaluate positive and negative aspects of its meetings ... Education is important: make it a priority in the meetings ... Teach the meaning behind the words, and different ways of applying it to a Masonic Life" [etc.]

These two articles are full of "food for thought" and are good candidates for serious discussions in our Lodges.

Last, but not least, is *The Word*. We receive it every month. And it includes at least one or two articles that bring up important topics. In the latest issue (September 2019, p.2) there is an essay written by a recently raised Brother, which is full of candor and good thoughts.

Essay says:

> "Education, may not always need be an esoteric discussion ... it could also develop a discussion about things in the community that need our help ... Is it possible to talk about current issues, without slipping into political division? ... This is necessary to making masonry relevant in our lives, as well as into our respective communities"; "A vision for the Lodge must be formed, and then implemented ... Go to Lodge, stand up, and make known what kind you want!" [etc.]

We could read this essay, and then discuss it in open Lodge, as Education material.

All these thoughts remind this Mentor of his Essay to the Masonic Renewal Committee's 2018 Bedwell Memorial Competition. Titled *What is the Purpose of the Masonic Fraternity, Now and in the Future*, it is in http://web.cortland.edu/romeu/mybedwellessay2018.pdf. In it, we writes:

> "Any organization acquires, with its members, an unwritten contract to make good use of their time and resources... Some join to improve themselves — and some of these, to help improve society at large... One way to increase our visibility is by developing community projects... Community work will also be the best promotion of our Craft."

Such will help us grow!

Jorge L. Romeu
Onondaga District Mentoring Chair

The Mentoring Corner

October 2019

Hello, Brethren!

The last weekend of September, the NY Scottish Rite COD was held in Syracuse. Several GLNY Grand Officers were in attendance, including our Grand Master and his Deputy. Presentations on recruitment of new members, an effort where both Grand Lodge and Scottish Rite have invested much time, effort and money creating videos, CDs and web pages, were given.

Speakers discussed the objectives, summarized in the Three Rs: *Recruit, Retain and Rejoin*. On recruiting, interested profanes fill a web contact form that is sent to the district mentoring chairs. We contact these individuals and invite them to meet with a Lodge NorthStar officer. About half of the times, I do not get any response from these individuals. Those that reply to our invitation are processed through NorthStar, and most become Masons. The critical work starts there.

Our main issue is *Retainment [Retention]*. After being raised, these new Brothers start attending Lodge. But in many cases, they confront the Three Bs: *Banality* (discussing payments), *Bickering* (fighting for nothing), that creates *Boredom* (difference between their expectations and realizations). Such can lead to a *Demit* or an *NPD* [Non-Payment of Dues]. All the efforts expended in member Recruitment is then forever lost.

To explore the origins of their dissatisfaction we need to consider *some reasons to join the Craft*, all legitimate, but different. Some people join for our *Fellowship*; others, for our *esoterism*; or for the *safety net and support* they acquire, as members of the Craft, if they endure problems. Others join to *improve themselves*, or to *help others* improve their lot. This latter group experiences the largest disappointment, as the associated activities are undertaken poorly, seldom, or not at all.

There is modest Masonic Education in some Lodges, or the topic is poorly chosen or developed. At times, the presenter speaks, while the audience sits passively listening; or presents a topic of little interest. Topics of wide interest, actively discussed, are much more effective and efficient.

Finally, some Brothers join to get involved with an organization that is active in the community, *and provides help to others. As Masons, we are taught with the 24 Inch Gauge, that the time of the day should be divided into three equal parts: for work, rest, and the service of God.* We are also taught that *he best serves God, who serves his Fellow men.* Some may shy away from taking part within society because they fear this will bring in *politics, a topic totally forbidden in Lodge.*

There is a big *difference between politics and policy*, which is not a forbidden topic. Let's offer an example. We currently have, without discussion, a large drug addiction problem. What are its causes, consequences, and health and economic impacts? Drug addiction is a *policy issue* and a legitimate Lodge topic. The different solutions to deal with it are a matter of *partisan politics.*

Policy issues are of interest not only to Lodge members, but also to relatives, friends, neighbors. Open the Lodge to our community! Find an exciting topic and a good speaker to present it! This may well help more to improve our recruitment, retention and rejoining, than any video or CD!

Jorge L. Romeu
Onondaga District Mentoring Chair

The Mentoring Corner

November 2019

Hello, Brethren!

The last Friday of October we had, as on every year, our District Convention. I always attend, for I learn much; I have a chance to meet many Brothers from other Lodges, some are old friends, and others will become good friends; and of course, I get a free dinner! You can't beat that!

I still remember my first Convention, several years ago, at Jordan Lodge. As it started, the Grand Lecturer walked around the Lodge, and stopped in front of me. "Brother", he said, "please lend me your name badge". He took it to the WM and asked him: "What does it say here?" The WM answered. Then, the Grand Lecturer took it to the SW and the JW, and asked the same question. They also answered -or rather murdered my Hispanic name in several different ways. The Grand Lecturer then came back to my place, returned my badge, and turned around. He walked a couple of steps, stopped, and turned to me: "By the way, Brother, how do you pronounce your name?"

After I did, he said to the entire Lodge: "A name is a very important thing. Before you state a Candidate's name during a Degree, be sure you know how to pronounce it correctly."

This year's Convention was very instructive: we opened Lodge in First Degree; then we worked the first two Sections of the Ritual of Initiation. The Grand Lecturer explained all the whys and the hows of the Degree elements. It was a great learning experience! RW Harvey Easman, who has been around for a long time, said this Convention was as good as the best he has ever seen.

Then, the Grand Lecturer started discussing the importance of Ritual work, and of Lodge work in general. He said, and in the opinion of this Mentor, rightly so, that deficient Lodge work is one of the main causes of Demits and NPDs. Poor Lodge work negatively affects Retention. Thence, it is necessary to start improving on this, if we want the current Recruiting efforts to yield fruit.

This Mentor is, by trade and training, a statistician. We collected data from one of our District Lodges, no different than any other, and implemented a Pilot "Survival Analysis". We looked into "time to Demit/NPD" for the 90 Brothers initiated from year 2000 to 2019. Average Demit occurs 5 years from Initiation date. More than half of all Brothers Initiated since the year 2000, have by now already Demitted/NPD; 13% of those that Demitted did not even go beyond First Degree. The analysis is in the Web: https://web.cortland.edu/romeu/LodgAnalYrstoDemit.pdf

In layman's terms: if Initiations were sales, and Demits/NPD were returns, this Lodge had 51 returns out of its 90 sales! A Merchant would rather have 20 sales and one return. This Mentor is willing and able to redo this analysis, by including more Lodges, and possibly more information about the Brothers: age, status (married, single), etc.. Such information can then be used to detect factors that affect (increase/decrease) time to Demit, in a similar way as a patient's age, gender, disease phase, etc., are used, in cancer research, to determine time to death and influence factors.

Only by identifying the causes, can we work on them, and fix them, or at least reduce them.

Jorge L. Romeu

Onondaga District Mentoring Chair

The Mentoring Corner

December 2019

Hello, Brethren:

As I write this column, the year is coming to an end. Holiday and family gatherings and parties, are in order. It is a good time to look back and reflect about what we have accomplished.

Our main concern this year, as a Mentor and member of The Craft, has been on Recruiting and Retaining (R&R) activities. Apparently, most institutions suffer from poor attendance and reduced membership, especially among the young, who leave their churches and religions in alarming numbers. Pew Research Center's survey (2018-19) results show that 64% of Millenials (born 1981-96) attend a few times a year, or none. My own *pilot study* showed that 56% of all Brethren, Initiated from the year 2000 onward in the Lodge we studied, were no longer members.

To deal with the R&R issue, Grand Lodge and Scottish Rite have developed R&R CDs, videos and web pages. Another approach is to *develop more Open activities* that connect Lodges to their surrounding communities. In many cases, our neighbors don't know there is a Lodge, or may be intimidated to attend; they ignore what we do, and often have questionable information.

We tried this approach in our own Lodge: writing an article on polls and surveys, a hot topic https://www.syracuse.com/opinion/2019/11/statistics-expert-how-to-make-sense-of-political-polls-commentary.html, advertising the Lodge event in the newspaper, and had coffee and cake. Nobody showed up. It was on the same night of Presidential debates and Impeachment hearings.

Wor. John Bromka, of Morningstar Lodge, Marcellus, also organized an *open event*, with Bro. Ed Stone's Pearl Harbor presentation. They had approximately 40 attendees (room capacity was 49), of which about 1/3 were Masons, 1/3 were congregants of St John's church (where some Lodge members attend), and 1/3 came from personal invitations. Wor. Bromka filled online Post Standard and Eagle/Pennysaver forms, but neither newspaper printed anything. On Monday, Feb. 4th, Morningstar will host RW David Menegon presentation *Freemasonry, the Cornerstone to Civil Society, and how our principles rebuild communities and countries*. RW Menegon is in the Speakers Roster: http://suffolkmasons.com/glofny-launching-new-speakers-bureau-website/ [page unavailable].

A third example is the monthly presentation series that the Livingston Library of our Grand Lodge is conducting. Many New York Masons have discussed interesting topics about The Craft, which are taped and can be accessed through: https://nymasoniclibrary.org/youtube-channel/ This is another excellent source for great programs, that can be shown in our Lodges for free.

We can extract several lessons from these. First, a good topic is OK, and so is advertising in local media; but this is not sufficient. To draw an audience, we also need to have the support of our Lodge members, and of their families, and also our friends and neighbors. This worked like a charm for Morningstar. Livingston Library has built a following by having their functions on a regular basis. A one-time event is easily missed, and it does not build a continual following.

The Word serves four Masonic Districts, with several hundred brothers. Hence, we could find enjoyable presenters to discuss interesting topics in a District Lodge, every month. We could also draw speakers from the Grand Lodge Roster. The talks could rotate among Lodges and Districts. Well advertised, with support from our own, rooms could fill up with attendees. It is worth a try!

As our neighbors get to know us better, some may become interested in joining us. They will also recognize Freemasonry as a community asset. RW Menegon will talk on how Freemasonry is a vibrant part of Civil Society, and can help rebuild our communities. It will be a useful talk.

Jorge L. Romeu
Onondaga District Mentoring Chair

2020

The Mentoring Corner

January 2020

Hello, Brethren:

As I do every time I drive to Florida, I visit my Mentor and tell him what I am working on. I told him about trying to make the Lodge more relevant to the community it is inserted in. And how I ineffectively tried to give an open talk on a general topic, for the community we belong to.

My Mentor said that today it is difficult to find an area to work on. With unemployment and health insurance people don't need the material support Lodges provided a century ago. The Education is provided by public school systems. Cell phones and the Internet allows us to obtain information and socialize without leaving the comfort of our own homes.

I explained to him that, in spite of all these modern advances, there was still room for us to provide useful input to the society where we insert our Lodges; to be useful to it; to be an asset.

Health insurance will pay for medical treatment, but will never send anyone a post card, visit them to cheer them up, take them out ...Unemployment will provide for their physical needs, not their spiritual ones... School is excellent to obtain knowledge and study a career, but it will not give food for the soul. Cell phones and email cannot substitute the warmth of a human. All of this can be summarized in a single word, of great importance in The Craft: **Fellowship**. Fads will come and go; but in the end, humans will always prefer the interaction with other humans.

In addition, we have several other important contributions for the society where we interact. First, there is our proverbial **tolerance and brotherly love**. In these challenging days we live in, where many tend to side and interact only with those who share their ideas, and dismiss all others as aliens. People need to relearn how to disagree without being disagreeable; to be more tolerant of each other; and to remember that we are all brothers and sisters, under the eyes of God. We can provide both, the good example, and the activities that foster such tolerant behavior.

Finally, we have many senior members in our Lodges that have spent their lives working in different fields. They have acquired valuable experiences that should not be lost. They can be transmitted to our younger generations. We need to find ways of doing so.

In recent years, Grand Lodge has spent much effort and resources creating websites, CDs, flyers, etc., to attract new members to The Craft. There are, today, only 10% of the members that the Craft had just after the Second World War. Similar situation occurs with other Grand Lodges, with churches, with clubs and professional societies. It is a sign of the times.

As Mentoring Chair for the District I receive the NorthStar information from many prospects that access such website. I pass them to our Lodges. About half of them never follow through. In a pilot study I conducted in one of our Lodges, more than half of those Brothers initiated between 2000 and 2019, had left The Craft after five years. We need to work on Masonic Education, and Lodge programs and activities. We need to become relevant in our communities; we can become assets and some neighbors may become interested.

In the mid-1800s, after the Morgan Affair and the creation of the Anti-Masonic party, many hundreds of New York Lodges were closed, and thousands of Masons demitted. But after the storm passed, The Craft came back, stronger. We just need to make better Masons and become more relevant in our communities, and the Sun will also come out for us.

We recently had a very successful Town Hall for Grand Line Candidates, in an atmosphere of respect and fraternity. Candidates presented their visions and answered many of our questions.

Jorge L. Romeu
Onondaga District Mentoring Chair

The Mentoring Corner

February 2020

Hello, Brethren:

Once upon a time, a good Brother went through some serious financial problems, and sought the aid of Deity. He thus prayed: "My God, I have always been your faithful servant; I have kept your commands, loved and cared for my family and been a good person. I am now behind in my mortgage and car payments because I am helping my son pay his college tuition. I need to win the Lotto number. Please God, help me out!" The whole week passed and he did not win. So he prayed again in the same manner. And nothing happened. He thus went on, for several weeks. He finally got a little mad, and again prayed: "My God, I am very frustrated! I implored you and requested your help, in desperation. And you have ignored my Plight!" At this time, a solemn voice from heaven answered him: "But Joe, you must, at least, buy a Lottery Ticket!"

The lesson behind this story is that good intentions, by themselves, are not enough. We need to accompany them with practical and effective actions. And so it occurs, with our beloved Craft.

We talk, write and complain about how we are losing members. But, what are we doing? Do we attend Lodge regularly? Do we actively participate in Committees and other activities? Do we help create, advertise, and then participate in the Lodge programs presented?

This month, a Masonic Conference was scheduled in Auburn, organized by the four CNY Districts. It was canceled because there was not enough attendance to make it possible. Morning Star Lodge put together a Burns Dinner Table Lodge; only nine Brethren showed up. And so on.

Masters, Wardens, and Deacons association seldom meets. Their meetings allow Leaders of our Lodges to share ideas, plan, advertise and support joint meetings and other functions. Costs of such events could be partially underwritten by all Lodges, in a manner similar to Investitures, helping to increase attendance. Our four CNY Districts have around forty Lodges. One attendee from each Lodge would not only provide our events with a critical mass, but could also give a short presentation, at his return to his Lodge, thereby enticing others to attend future events.

Grand Line Town Hall, Grand Lecturer's Convention, and other important events that used to attract well over a hundred Brethren, barely bring half that many, today. Joint events put in contact the most active Brethren in our Lodges, increasing their interaction and making possible that they plan, organize and support District-wide events. The Syracuse Valley of Scottish Rite is an example of such organization. Many CNY District DDGMs and Staff Officers are members, and can discuss there, how to support each other, scheduling and organizing District functions.

We also need to start using modern methods, such as Teleconferences, in our Masonic work. These allow several individuals that are in different locations to have a joint conversation, as if they were in the same room. In addition, we can email a PowerPoint presentation, that each of the participants can view. Teleconferences can then be used for training and Masonic Education. Teleconferencing may allow Lodges to work during winter, when the weather does not cooperate and some Lodges go Dark. Telecon phone numbers can be obtained free of cost; their cost free use is easy to learn. Oswego District Staff Officer has used Teleconferences successfully.

Every organization needs a Core group: a small motor that helps start the larger motor. But such Core group does not develop by spontaneous generation. It has to be fostered. and nurtured. The Core group also needs a place where they periodically meet and befriend each other.

Creation and fostering of such Core group could well be how we "buy our Lottery ticket".

Jorge L. Romeu
Onondaga District Mentoring Chair

The Mentoring Corner
March 2020

Hello, Brethren:

This Mentor has been an observer of the Craft for many years (in Cuba, PR, and the US) with the objective of understanding it (and thus serving it) better. As a result, we have arrived to the conclusion that there exist, at least, four different types of Lodge Members. Understanding this question, and planning our activities accordingly, may result in attaining more effective results.

One type of Lodge Member seldom attends. Some participated many years ago, but are now old, sick, or living in another state. Some others may be young, struggling to build a family and a business. Both pay their dues, adhere to, and support, even silently, our Institution's principles. The older ones have already contributed. The second group eventually will — when their life and circumstances allow them to. Keep in touch with, and update these members, and leave them be.

Another Member type enjoys and seeks fellowship and socialization. They attend regularly as side-liners to Lodge meetings. They are our Ruffians, Conductors and other required elements of Degree work. They join Committees, and the Line, but without intending to become Deacons or Wardens — let alone, Lodge Masters. Such Brethren are extremely useful: encourage and help them grow Masonically. When ready, these Brethren will take more challenging responsibilities.

Another type seeks higher levels of Lodge responsibility and leadership, such as Wardens and Masters. With time, they may seek higher levels: as AGLs, Staff Officers and even DDGMs. They may eventually become Grand Lodge officers. Encourage, groom, educate, and support them, for our Craft needs good leaders! Grand Lodge has excellent leadership offerings, such as the The 24 Inch Gauge course. And the Livingston Library has several useful books and courses.

Another type of Brethren is interested in specialized aspects of the Craft, such as esoteric, ritualistic or historical studies, so necessary to better understand our Institution and its work. Grand Lodge already has Research and Ritual Lodges. Encourage these Brethren to join them.

There may be other types of Masons that I have not identified here; plus the natural mixing of the above classes, such as Leaders, with strong ritual or esoteric interests, and so on.

Any organization, and our Craft is surely a good example, needs different types of members to help it advance and develop — in the same way that a garden needs different types of flowers and plants to be beautiful. Member inclinations should be identified and encouraged, starting at their Initiation. Once identified, they could be encouraged to follow their heart. They could also be assigned a Mentor, to prepare and help them join up a group of similarly inclined Brethren.

In a previous column, we talked about the creation and fostering of Core Groups in Lodge, that could work as the small motor that helps start the big one. Such groups do not need to be exclusively for fostering administrative leaders. They could also include other activities: social, ritual, education, history, crafts, community participation, etc.. Side Liners, and Brethren that are currently not attending, or that are scarcely participating in Lodge activities, may discover a group that fits their inclinations, and may want to join them, thus becoming more active.

Finding convenient schedules for these groups to meet, whether in Lodge or in other places of their choice, would also help. It is possible to work in informal settings: while shooting pool, playing cards or Bingo, or watching a good program, or video. An enjoyable discussion of the material presented in such gatherings is always productive. John Dewey, the eminent American educator, proposed that *people best learn by doing*, especially with a *challenging, joint project*!

Jorge L. Romeu
Onondaga District Mentoring Chair

The Mentoring Corner
April 2020

Hello, Brethren:

We are all facing exceptional circumstances: the scourge of the Coronavarus Pandemia. Our way of life has been drastically changed: Social Distancing: We have to stay inside as much as we can. Go out only to shop for the essentials, to avoid infection. Listen to the daily reports about how the Virus is moving throughout our county, state, country and world! And wait ...

Our children and grandchildren are in another state. We contact them daily through Internet and phone: FaceTime, teleconferencing, etc.. We recognize the importance of togetherness ...

My wife and I are teaching by Distance Learning. No more tests; only group homework that is then reviewed through Face-

Time. No graduation; no church or Lodge gatherings; everything online...

My wife says: "now I have you for myself; you can't go to school to teach, to church to sing or to the Lodge!" We now spend all day long together, like when we started, fifty years ago ...

We talk two or three times a day with our sons, using software video facilities. We have a seven-month-old grandson who is now learning to crawl. We have a 24 year old grandson, in college; and everything in-between. We use classroom Software to share both video and voice (one of the perks of being a teacher). The important thing is to keep in close contact, even at a distance.

So, what should Masons do? As MWGM Sardone said: **Freemasonry doesn't stop!**

As Mentoring Chair, we are conducting a One-hour Teleconference every Monday at 8 pm. We read an article related to Freemasonry, appropriate for Masons and non-Masons, and we talk about the topic. The **Telecon Phone No: 605-475-4831, with access code 710272.**

I hang in the Web the material that I will discuss, so Brethren can view it while I present. In the past three Mondays we have discussed: (1) Freemasonry in Encyclopedia Britannica articles; (2) analysis of Craft membership in UK and USA; (3) 300th anniversary of the foundation of the Grand Lodge of London and its impact on Civil Society, given at the Livingston Library, and that you can view in YouTube: https://www.youtube.com/watch?v=31rUnNsOlfk&t=1999s

There are many excellent articles in the website of Grand Lodge of British Columbia, CA: https://freemasonry.bcy.ca/

texts/ and the George Washington Masonic Memorial Light magazine is available in: https://gwmemorial.org/pages/light

If you are a Scottish Rite member, the AASR has a new Internet facility that we can use. We first need to register, which is very easy. Go to: https://id.scottishritenmj.org/mds/Register/

It is good to keep our mind in topics other than Coronavirus. Many public libraries offer books online. Onondaga County's website is: https://www.onlib.org/find/e-books-and-more

We can also read web newspapers, watch videos in YouTube, contact our relatives by email, watch a movie, or one of the Travel shows in PBS. Or simply, read an old-fashion paper book.

These are hard times, and most of us have to be isolated in our homes to prevent infection of the virus. This situation will last for some time. Until it is safe, we better keep to ourselves.

But this situation also presents an opportunity to serve both the Craft and our broader community. We can volunteer, through Grand Lodge or our District DDGM, to contact brothers and give of our professional experience (e.g. accounting, psychology etc.). We can also offer our abilities to local authorities. This would let people know we exist and contribute.

And, most of all, let's keep our spirits up. There is a God. The GAOTU will provide.

Jorge L. Romeu
Onondaga District Mentoring Chair

The Mentoring Corner

May 2020

Hello, Brethren:

The Coronavirus Pandemia, now officially named COVID-19, continues to ravage the country and the world. At this time, there are at least 250,000 deaths worldwide, 70,000 in the US, and 20,000 in New York State. We are locked down, with most economic activity closed, many lost jobs, etc..

This provides The Craft, one of the largest, oldest members of Civil Society, with a well-connected state-wide organization and valuable Social Capital, a chance to serve itself as well as the community. As retirees, we don't need to worry about losing our jobs. We regularly receive a retirement check, and have available free time. Many activities can be implemented through the Internet, without exposing anyone to contagion. There is much good we can do, which will bring The Craft appreciation. Some Lodges have already started volunteering to help both our brothers and our communities. Such activities let people know that Freemasonry exists and contributes.

For example, through the *Weekly Masonic Update* of Western NY Research Lodge, we learned how several Brothers organized curb-side donations for food pantries. And through *Hiram's Highlights*, we found that MWGM Sardone arranged for a Lender Advisor to discuss financial problems, and that RW Friedman embarks on a Monday lectures series, on Leadership.

The Scottish Rite runs a series of Video Degree Confers, on Thursday nights, which are seldom offered due to their size and complexity. This Mentor has already taken three of these degrees. We assume that the York Rite is also offering interesting and useful Internet activities.

It is also good to explore new avenues of entertainment. Netflix includes many foreign films and TV Series. We have viewed several detective series from Swedish, Polish, Belgian, Italian, and

Icelandic TV, similar to *Dr. Blake's Mysteries* that NPR, the public TV station, has offered.

Such TV programs also show us how life takes place in other countries, and what these look like. For example, we looked up Iceland in Wikipedia, and found that it was a Danish territory until 1944, and has since become one of the wealthiest and most developed nations in the world.

It is good to keep busy with activities unrelated to Coronavirus, to uplift our state of mind and renew our ideas. We are in for a long haul. If the 1918 Pandemic serves as model, there may be more than one wave coming. Older people are at higher risk, so our Lodges will need in order to maintain Social Distancing, to re-develop some of its functions online. We must re-invent Masonry just as broader society must reinvent workplaces, schools, and public transportation.

Recently we have received an Edict from MWGM Sardone, extending Lodge officers' time until we can safely meet again to elect new officers. Maintaining Social Distancing is difficult within a Lodge room, even wearing masks. Meeting outdoors in a park, for a picnic, or in smaller Lodge subgroups, may become good alternatives. We will find ways to safely socialize again.

Regarding Mentoring, we continue to receive emails from NorthStar, with the names of persons interested in Freemasonry. We continue sending them emails, explaining how NorthStar works, providing some Masonic information sites, and asking them to respond to us with their concerns. Not many candidates reply to our emails. Some don't even include their home address in their interest form. This gives the impression that some hits come from individuals satisfying their curiosity about Freemasonry. But that they are not really interested in joining us. Those who do respond to follow up emails and show some interest are thence passed along to Lodges.

Freemasonry will continue to work throughout these difficult times: differently but surely!

Jorge L. Romeu
Onondaga District Mentoring Chair

The Mentoring Corner

August 2020

Hello, Brethren:

A Chinese proverb says: may you live in interesting times. And under such we currently are!

The Coronavirus Pandemic continues to ravage our country and the world. The number of deaths worldwide as well as in the US have doubled in two months. We are no longer locked down in NYS; but several other states are considering, or implementing again, such practices.

This provides *The Craft*, one of the largest and oldest members of *Civil Society*, a chance to serve itself, as well as its community. Many activities have been implemented throughout this time: some in person, others in the Internet. For example, some Lodges have helped distribute food; others have organized food drives. The Grand Master has organized Zoom presentations on economics, health, sports and, most recently, the Masonic Medical Research Institute. The Grand Lodge of Puerto Rico has directed its Lodges to help with contact tracing. This mentor has been (https://www.researchgate.net/publication/343345908_A_Markov_Model_to_Study_Covid-19_Herd_Immunization) developing models to better understand COVID-19 problems. Each one of us can do something to help in this struggle, which will earn The Craft valued appreciation.

But community involvement brings back the old debate between *activism and introspection. Introspection* states that a Freemason should search God. And if his faith induces him to follow a public course of action, he shall do so on his own, independently of the Craft. *Activism* assumes the Craft is a member of *Civil Society*, and *has a non-partisan role* to play in our communities. American Freemasonry is closer to Introspection. Spanish Caribbean Freemasonry is closer to Activism. Article 1 of the Grand Lodges of Cuba and Puerto Rico states: "Freemasonry is the Institution of Morality. Its goals include: eradication of ignorance, combating vice, and inspiring the Love for Humanity". Those goals *encourage* active, non-partisan, *community involvement*.

A happy medium between these two positions could be found. Especially in times like these, where we can see the world crumbling around us: people dying and losing their jobs by the thousands; and our country, more divided in more than one way, than I have ever seen before.

The Craft is the Institution of Brotherly Love and Tolerance, two of the most important but absent elements, in our days. We see mistrust, acrimony and ill faith all over. Such will not help resolve the severe health and economic crisis created by COVID-19. A voice of moderation is desperately needed. Freemasonry is especially endowed to help such a voice re-emerge.

We *Masons come in all sizes and colors*. There are young and old Brethren; rich and poor; white and black; working and retired. We come from all political persuasions, religions, trades and professions. We can *start by having*, and perhaps inviting others to have, a civil conversation about the important issues that affect us all, where *all participants express themselves* openly, in an urbane manner, without fear of being labeled. A real conversation can only take place when *all participants* are able to *present their positions, and explain their arguments*. The media (radio, TV, newspapers) are generally as polarized as the rest of us, which only helps inflame the situation and complicate its solution. These are just some of the areas that need hard work.

How can we, as Masons, contribute? Should we? If so, in what way? These are all difficult questions. But the very *first thing* should be to *start talking* about it. If we, *Masons, can find a way to address these issues judiciously*, then we may be able to *show others* a way to do it, too.

Jorge L. Romeu
Onondaga District Mentoring Chair

The Mentoring Corner

September 2020

Hello, Brethren:

The Coronavarus Pandemic continues ravaging our country and the world. The number of deaths in the US is close to 200,000, and the COVID-19 cases are over six million. This national emergency provides The Craft with a chance to serve itself, as well as its community. In past national emergencies our Craft has done this. For example, in the last issue of *The Word*, an August 1919 article in *The Builder* was reproduced, regarding Masonic aid during World War I:

... the conference at Cedar Rapids reports on the Overseas Mission in which Judge Scudder, a Justice of the Supreme Court of New York, and a most scholarly and forward looking brother, recited to those present the details of the negotiations with the government, looking to the fraternity being recognized as one of the official agencies engaged in welfare work among the men of the army and navy overseas. The Masonry of the United States was so recognized by the War Department, the activities in which it proposed to engage were approved ...

The Craft today is still in capacity to contribute. Actually, much has already been done, both individually and as an Institution (see our article of last month). But there is more we can still do. Lodges and Brethren can come up with better ideas than I can suggest, here, for self help, as well as to contribute to the broader communities where we have inserted our Lodges.

We are heading into Fall and Lodge attendance is an issue. There is not yet a treatment or vaccine for COVID-19. Some of us are in high risk groups (age, co-morbidities) while others are not. Those who can attend Lodge meetings should. Those who have health concerns can find other ways to participate (Zoom programs, readings, etc). There are excellent, free tutorials in the web to learn how to use them: https://zoom.us/resources; https://support.zoom.us/hc/en-us/articles/217214286-Watch-Recorded-Training-Sessions; and https://support.zoom.us/hc/en-us/articles/206618765-Zoom-video-tutorials; are some. We can also find tutorials in YouTube.

This is also good time to re-read degrees in the Liturgy, especially the Charges. And to think through all this material that either went too fast when we first read them or it was a long time ago, and we have forgotten. It is also a good time to re-read the 24 Inch Gage manual, for those of us who have been Masters, or those Brethren who are in the Line and will eventually become one. Informal study groups for all these topics could be formed using Zoom or Free Conference phone accounts. Also, while the weather is good, Lodges could arrange outdoors gatherings in parks or backyards, so we could keep in touch. Open spaces always provide for better venues.

We can also remain in touch through the Internet: email, chat, web pages, Facebook, etc.. We can access them from our home computers and interact, learn, listen to talks, etc.. Grand Lodge of Puerto Rico organized three and four evening presentations per week, during summer. And we can do likewise, in our District, at Grand Lodge level, or both. The thing is to keep active under the new operating rules until we can return to our past, usual activities. However, I am concerned that, even after a vaccine and a treatment are found, things will never return to what they were, before the COVID-19 pandemic started. If so, we will have to permanently adapt to new forms.

This is fine. Freemasonry has successfully evolved, during its 300+ years of existence!

Jorge L. Romeu
Onondaga District Mentoring Chair

The Mentoring Corner
October 2020

Hello, Brethren:

COVID-19 continues affecting our daily lives. For example, we visited, as we do every summer, our grandchildren in Florida. But this year our road trip was completely different.

Interstate I-95 was unusually empty for this time of the year. With relatively few cars on the road, motel reservations were not required; breakfast was no longer provided; people wore masks and kept their distance wherever we stopped for gas or food; and most services were take-out.

Melbourne is similar to Syracuse: a small city with low infection rate. So our stay was very relaxed: visiting with family, going to the beach, or for walks, and occasionally going to a store.

I tried visiting the local Lodge to meet with my Mentor, as I always do when I travel there. He called me to say that two Brothers had tested positive for COVID-19, so the Lodge canceled its meetings, to avoid a potential spread of the Virus among Brethren. At our return to Syracuse we spent two weeks in quarantine, to avoid potentially spreading the virus to others, in case we had become infected during our trip out of state. We want to keep community spread rate low.

Last week President Trump also tested positive for COVID-19 and was admitted to the Naval Hospital for a few of days. In addition, a dozen other White House staffers also tested positive.

So, what does all of that imply, for us, as Masons? *Freemasonry is a state of mind.* Even if we are unable to attend Lodge, we remain as such. Our basic tenet is: *Freemasonry never stops.*

THE MENTORING CORNER ~ 135

During the summer we attended many Internet and outdoor Masonic activities: virtual talks, some from other jurisdictions; several Zoom programs sponsored by Grand Lodge — two of them on COVID-19, presented by MMRI staff and, also via Zoom, several Scottish Rite Degrees. Then, Livingston Library is offering excellent monthly virtual lectures: https://nymasoniclibrary.org/

COVID-19 is going to be around, for a while. The CDC has prescribed five rules to enhance our safety: wash hands often, keep social distance, wear a mask when in public, prefer open to closed spaces, and avoid crowded gatherings. This is especially important for High Risk groups.

Many Masons are 65 years of age or older; Lodges are closed spaces; meetings are long and include several (sometimes many) Brethren. Some of us may feel concerned if we attend ...

But this doesn't mean that our Masonic participation will diminish; it will only change form. We can always meet via Zoom, to keep in touch and to develop interesting programs. This is the perfect moment to study those Masonic topics that we have been putting aside, for lack of time.

Take a book from the Lodge library, or select an article from The Word, or from a Masonic website. Form a group of interested Brethren to *read and discuss* the material. Maybe DDGM could help organize such groups and The Word could advertise meeting times. These types of activities will help us *grow Masonically*, as well as to increase our circle of friends. For, we often start by talking about, say a book, and end up talking about many other more engaging things.

Small Groups could occasionally gather in open spaces, such as Green Lakes, to walk and enjoy the changing colors of the Fall, or the snowed pine trees, in Winter, and *talk Freemasonry*.

And during these walks and talks, we could plan activities to support our communities, help those in need, and make *our friends and neighbors aware of Freemasonry*. It is in times like this that individuals and organizations can carry out their service to God, and to their fellow humans.

It is said that *Masonry takes some good men and makes them better*. And *some* of these men still want to *walk the extra mile*. Let's encourage and *help* them do so!

Jorge L. Romeu
Onondaga District Mentoring Chair

The Mentoring Corner

November 2020

Hello, Brethren:

The Presidential election is just over. The winner is not yet known, for results are very close (vote counting is still on). Our Nation is split in half, regarding the voting. But what is shocking is that each side tends to look at the other side as the adversary. In a recent Economist poll (X/31/20; p. 22), 60% of US voters think that members of the other party constitute a threat to America. A WSJ map (XI/5/20; p. A6) shows predominance of one party in large cities, and of the other party, in small ones and in rural areas. Then, the tone of public discourse is very harsh, which does not help in finding solutions to our problems, and is replicated in the national Media.

For example, in a recent TV political show, one of the participants said that those who voted for the opposing candidate did not do the right thing. Such statement suggests a lack of tolerance. The TV participant should assume that, just as he most likely does, people who vote for the other candidate are also voting their conscience. And voting one's conscience is the right thing to do.

Such unfortunate state of affairs offers the Craft *an opportunity to help restore the tone of public discourse by sharing our two most important pillars: tolerance and brotherly love.* Some will say *Freemasonry should not be concerned with politics.* I certainly agree that we should not meddle in *partisan politics.* But *defusing the partisan bias* that is tearing our country apart is not! It is a *wonderful opportunity to both serve it, and showcase our fundamental Masonic traits!*

Several years ago, when I started attending Liverpool Syracuse Lodge, a likeness of George Washington was displayed at its front porch, with a notice saying: Washington was a Mason. Houdini was a Mason — and so was I. But neither could convey to the general public what our Institution stood for, as Washington did: *character, duty, compromise with God and country.*

Tolerance encourages us to think that people are basically honest. Differences in Thought, therefore, must stem from *different assessments of the issues.* Discussing such differences with respect, could help restore harmony. *Three approaches* come to mind, to help implement them:

We can have a Speaker address an issue, followed by a Q&A from the public. We can also organize a Panel of two or three speakers, presenting different viewpoints. Give each speaker 10 minutes to establish their position, and then engage in thoughtful and respectful debate. Thirdly, a Town Hall format, whereby a Moderator sets the topic, enforces participation rules, and directs the debate. Non-partisan topics such as polls, the Electoral

College or voting by mail, could be chosen. The lessons from the debate option would not be about topics, as about validating that it is *possible to disagree* and present different views *without becoming disagreeable or pugnacious*.

Such sessions could be carried out live, in Lodge premises, or via Zoom, to avoid potential health issues. Lodge Brothers, their families and friends would be encouraged to attend. It would also be publicized in the local media, so that community members could join in and participate.

What would the Craft gain from all this? *Public recognition* for its commitment to serve the community in which it is inserted! This may also encourage the desire among some neighbors, to join an organization committed to such positive values and to the community to which it belongs.

Some may argue that the Craft is an organization that serves its members. A century ago, when life was more difficult, relief was a very strong reason to join. But today, most people have life, health, car and home insurance. Social Security and unemployment helps if we stop working Joining the Craft for its support is no longer as strong as it used to be. We need something more.

Jorge L. Romeu
Onondaga District Mentoring Chair

The Mentoring Corner

December 2020

Hello, Brethren:

We present a report on the NorthStar activities in Onondaga District. Earlier in November, I wrote a letter to our Worshipful

Masters and Secretaries requesting their Lodge results in processing candidates that Grand Lodge sent to our District (to me). I first contacted each candidate and told them about the North-Star. Then I asked them to reply if they were still interested in joining us. If Candidates answered positively (about half), they were assigned to a Lodge. Below, are the responses I received from our Lodges, regarding results they obtained.

From Bro. Chris Heberle, of the Northstar Program Committee for Nortrip Lodge No. 998, Fayetteville: Number of Candidates referred via the Northstar Program in the year 2020: Four; Number of which that have become Lodge members (1st, 2nd or 3rd Degrees) in 2020: Zero.

From, WM John Bromko of Morningstar Lodge No. 524: We are planning initiation Monday Dec 1, with candidate you forwarded us. I have been in communication with him since August.

From WM Brian Courtney, Crossroads United Lodge No. 93: we had at least 11 possible candidates and 2 responded regularly, and we met with them. Only one actually filled out his application form and NorthStar background check. He was voted in, this past Thursday. The depressing part is the time spent emailing, texting and calling these candidates, have them respond once, and then never hear from them again after multiple attempts.

The above comments, multiplied by the fourteen District Lodges, are also applicable to our work as NorthStar chair. We do not complain, as this is part of our job. But it reveals some of the issues with the Web Page approach: every web **hit** is sent by GL to the corresponding Districts. In these COVID-19 times, some people may browse the web and query the GL NorthStar page for sheer curiosity. But once they are contacted, and find out that they will undergo the NorthStar, and that they will need to submit personal info to our *WestGate* software, many of them vanish.

Another topic of importance are the several web talks in YouTube that have been created by Quatuor Coronati Correspondence Circle/ QCCC (https://www.quatuorcoronati.com/about-qc-lodge/membership/). Said Circle prints a yearly journal with the main talks presented to the Quatuor Coronati Lodge (https://www.quatuorcoronati.com/), the oldest research Lodge.

We can find them in the QCCC YouTube Channel, which includes many interesting lectures: https://www.youtube.com/channel/UCtym859NJOTDQ8OElaG945A/featured

For example, Bro. Prof. Andreas Onnefors talk about Masonic Diplomacy in London, around 1800 can be found in: https://www.youtube.com/watch?v=XrAEt_c_PSkBro. Prof. Ric Berman's presentation about modern Masonic rituals, was given at the GL of California, last year.

The video can be found in: https://www.youtube.com/watch?v=MJKGMmV95O8

Finally, Bro. Prof. Aubrey Newman's presentation on Grand Masters, Provincial Grand Masters, and Provincial Grand Lodges can be watched in: https://www.youtube.com/watch?v=Aj2i5braQj4 And there are several more .,.

These talks will help us increase our knowledge of The Craft. They may also motivate a few of us to get in contact, via Zoom, and create a discussion group to study them (and do likewise with The Word articles). Such, would be a good exercise, and a great opportunity to get together.

May the GAOTU keep us all safe, until we have the vaccine, and can again meet inside our Lodges. I wrote https://www.researchgate.net/publication/346305686_A_Digression_on_Covid-19_Vaccine_Clinical_Trials_and_its_Consequences an article about the vaccine and its process.

Jorge L. Romeu
Onondaga District Mentoring Chair

2021

The Mentoring Corner

January 2021

Hello, Brethren:

As we write this, we are still ruminating about the unacceptable events that took place in Washington DC, two days ago, when mobs invaded and vandalized the Capitol building. As a citizen, I cannot accept or justify such acts. As a Mason, my Obligation of Love of Country compels me to take action. This article tries to analyze the issue from a Masonic point of view.

This is not a political issue. Whether we support or antagonize President Trump, or we feel indifferent about him, we should be disturbed with the images of the Capitol we saw in our TV screens. Citizens have the right to peacefully protest, whatever their reasons are (be them about Black Lives Matter, or the Presidential Election results), and whether we agree with them or not (this falls into our Obligation to be Tolerant of others, especially of those who disagree with us).

But events have exposed that inside these protests there are at least two types of participants. Probably most are true believers in the justice of their protest. And these tend to be peaceful and lawful individuals. But a few others infiltrate these movements to advance their own interests, be them personal or political: to steal, vandalize or create problems. Brotherly Love Obligation does not cover those individuals. And it is precisely because of the latter, that we are contrived to act.

The Social Fabric is formed both by individuals, and by their organizations. The grouping of the latter is called Civil Society. Social Fabric provides unwritten laws that regulate the behavior of its members. We do not steal or kill because we are put in jail. We do not use foul language or take our clothes off in public because it is socially unacceptable: we are censured and ostracized.

The leaders of Civil Society could have made declarations or taken Ads in major newspapers condemning, in no uncertain terms, the entry and desecration of the Capitol building. The failure to publicly react to this unacceptable action signals their weakness and ineffectiveness.

A strong Civil Society response is far more than cosmetic. It sends a message to both our political leaders, and to individuals participating in protests. The former care about re-election, and will take into consideration voter's opinion. Good faith demonstrators will be more careful to join, and organizers will become aware of public rejection, which goes against their intent.

Freemasonry constitutes a special case. We are not just another irrelevant club. We are an Institution that prides itself in core principles such as Love of Country, Tolerance and Brotherly Love. Our principles, in addition to being Obligations, constitute a formal part of our laws and regulations. This latter and particular condition differentiates The Craft from other groups, and has both a positive and a negative side. The first side attracts good members: we want to belong to something noble. The second side is that, if our proclaimed Institutional values are seen by the outsiders as empty statements, they will portray Freemasonry in a very poor light. And that is not good for recruiting or retaining new members, or for self-image. We need to do something.

This Mentor proposes developing a series of simple Zoom presentations about a theme at the core of US founding: the Federalist Papers (https://guides.loc.gov/federalist-papers/full-text). They discuss the main concepts of the American Constitution, document that governs everything. But, how much do we actually know about these papers? How many were they? When were they written? Why? By whom? We could prepare a cycle of Zoom talks and open them to the public at large. This would provide The Craft good community exposure. If interested, send me an email.

May GAOTU keep us safe until we become vaccinated and can again meet in our Lodges.

Jorge L. Romeu
Onondaga District Mentoring Chair

The Mentoring Corner

February 2021

Hello, Brethren:

Last month, we wrote in our *The Word* column that Freemasonry is not just another club but an Institution based on certain key core principles including Love of Country, Tolerance and

Brotherly Love. We said that we needed to do something regarding the January 6 events. We proposed developing a series of Zoom presentations based on The Federalist Papers, document that discusses the main concepts of the American Constitution. We checked with several Grand Line and Scottish Rite officers, and received no concerns from any them — just a nice compliment. We obtained a Zoom reservation for Monday, February 1st, at 7 pm, to launch our first meeting.

We wrote a communication to the Officers of the four Central New York Masonic Districts covered by *The Word*. We asked them to circulate our invitation and Zoom link among Members of their constituent Lodges. Several DDGMs sent out the invitation and its link. We also sent the information to Logia La Fraternidad, a Hispanic Lodge in NYC that we often work with.

On Monday February 1st we had our first Zoom meeting, with 12 participants from NYC and CNY. I stated that the events of January 6th revealed we had a problem. But it also uncovered an opportunity. Losers get fixated in the problem; winners seize the opportunity. As Freemasons, we needed to address such opportunity using our core principles. We surely included supporters of all current political currents. But Masons hold a strong feeling of tolerance and love for each other, setting an example of Civility for society at large. After that, I read the Introduction.

We learned or reviewed how the Federalist Papers comprised 85 newspaper articles, written and published in New York City by Hamilton, Madison and Jay, between 1787 and 1788. Their objective was to convince readers to support the new American Constitution, soon to be ratified. Jay later became Chief Justice of the Supreme Court; Madison, President; Hamilton, Secretary of the Treasury in George Washington's cabinet. The Federalist

Papers constitutes the best written account of the US Constitution, which is the document that governs how we operate as a Nation.

Afterward, we had a short organizational meeting. It was decided to meet via Zoom on the First and Third Mondays of every month, at 7 pm. In our next meeting, on February 15th, Bro. George Reed will read Paper #1, which outlines the plan of the entire Federalist series. I have already secured, and sent again to the DGDMs, the Zoom link invitation that appears below:

> Jorge L Romeu is inviting you to a scheduled Zoom meeting February 15th at 7 pm:
> Join Zoom Meeting Link: https://syracuseuniversity.zoom.us/j/94173064005
> Meeting ID: 941 7306 4005; No Id or Password necessary. Just click on the link and enter.

When next *The Word* comes out above link will be outdated. The new link will look just like that. Invite your friends and neighbors, and share the Zoom information and link with your local library. It becomes an implicit recruitment activity. Remember Saint Francis preaching anecdote:

St. Francis invited a young priest to preach the Gospel. They left their Monastery early, and spent all day walking up and down the main streets, praying with their rosaries. After several hours in this, they returned to the Monastery. The young priest timidly asked: "I thought we were going to preach". To which St. Francis replied: "What do you think we have been doing all day?"

Jorge L. Romeu
Onondaga District Mentoring Chair

The Mentoring Corner
March 2021

Hello, Brethren:

If you have read this column during the past three issues of *The Word*, you already know there is a group of CNY Masons that meet, via Zoom, every first and third Mondays of the month, at 7 pm, to read one of *The Federalist Papers*. And if your Lodge belongs to a Masonic Districts that is forwarding such Zoom Links to its Lodges, and these are forwarding them to their members, you are also receiving the information required to log into these Zoom meetings.

So far, we have had four meetings (plus an extra one on the third Thursday, for the benefit of those Brothers interested in participating, but who are unable to do so due to AASR meetings on Mondays). We have read, so far, the Introduction, plus the first and second Federalist Papers. On March 15, Wor. James Rizzo, Master of Lake City Lodge No. 127, will read The Federalist Paper #6: *Concerning Dangers from Dissensions Between the States* (by A. Hamilton). The paper dwells on the weaknesses of human nature which may cause frequent and violent contests among the States unless a strong union is created. Even then, a lack of union constituted a danger to our Nation!

The objectives of such readings include: (1) learning the *rules of our democratic process*, as provided by the US Constitution, and (2) showing how, with *Brotherly Love and Tolerance*, it is possible for Brethren with different viewpoints to share and discuss information — a very useful lesson for many Americans, in these days of stressful contention, and of political intolerance.

Freemasonry is particularly positioned to allow the implementation of these ideas, given our core principles of Brotherly Love and Tolerance. However, Tolerance does not mean that one gives up their way of thinking, but that one accepts that there are others with different ways, and that, if we do not share these, we can argue our differences in a civil and constructive manner.

During these readings we also learned much about why The Federalist Papers were written, and about that political time. Then, thirteen American colonies joined to win Independence — but still needed to create one Nation. To achieve this, nine of these thirteen colonies had to ratify the Constitution, which would substitute the *Articles of Confederation*. New York State's support was crucial. Therefore, three patriots (Hamilton, Madison and Jay) decided to jointly publish a series of articles under the fictional name of Publius, to explain the need to adopt a Constitution. Evidently, their political climate was as contentious, and the in-fighting as crude, as it is now.

The Federalist Papers consisted of 85 articles. Our group is reading a selection of the best among them. If anyone is interested in joining us, but is not receiving information and the Link to do so, please send me an email [redacted] and I will be happy to comply.

Moving to another topic, we continue to receive, from Grand Lodge, the names of potential candidates to our Fraternity, who must undergo the NorthStar process. After being contacted by email, and being told that they will be assigned to a Lodge Mentor to follow such process, more than one half of said candidates never re-appear. But those who do, eventually join a Lodge.

COVID-19 vaccination is advancing. I had my shot today, and several other Brethren have already received at least their first doses. Vaccines can protect us from death or hospitalization. But we will still need to wear masks, keep social distancing, etc., as it is not known if the vaccines prevent asymptomatic illness, or virus transmission. The CDC has just come up with new safety rules for those who are vaccinated: small groups can meet in more informal settings. This means that we may soon be able to start meeting again, thereby attending Lodge in person.

Jorge L. Romeu
Onondaga District Mentoring Chair

The Mentoring Corner
April 2021

Hello, Brethren:

Some brothers may have noticed that some Masonic issues I raise are not typical. This observation is well taken. I come from the Spanish Caribbean Masonic tradition, which in some ways differs from the American one. (Our Freemasonry developed an important social and educational function.) I will illustrate such experience through an article I wrote some years ago: *Freemasonry in the Spanish Antilles during the Second Half of the XIX Century*, published in 2018, in Vol. 131 of the Masonic research journal *Ars Quatuor Coronatorum*.

I will reproduce several key paragraphs and statements therein, that speak for themselves:

"Spain invested in its rich Mexican and South American colonies spending very little time or capital in the Spanish Antilles ones. It was only after Spain lost all of its continental colonies that it started dedicating attention to its two remaining Caribbean colonies: Cuba and Puerto Rico.

Responsibility for Spain losing its Empire was not due to disloyal Cuban and Puerto Rican Creoles, to Freemasonry, or to American Imperialism, as some have claimed. It was due to the disastrous Spanish colonial policy, implemented throughout the XIX Century by its government.

Autochthonous Freemasonry (composed of Creole membership) provided the vehicle that allowed Cuban and Puerto Rican intellectuals and politicians to gather, interact, develop their skills and ideas, and bring to fruition their efforts to improve the governments of their islands.

In 1859, Grand Lodge of South Carolina, through Bros. Pike's and Mackey's intercession, provided charters enabling Cuban Bro. Andres Cassard to create the Grand Lodge of Colon. Bro. Cassard also created the Supreme Council of Colon, for Cuba and the Spanish Antilles.

In 1878, Cuba's first War of Independence ended with a Peace Treaty. In 1880, all Cuban Grand Lodges merged under Grand Master Antonio Govín, who was the President of the Liberal Autonomic Party. His key philosophy was that *Freemasonry would strive to obtain, by evolution, what had not been achieved by war*. Autonomist Party leadership included prominent members of Masonic Lodges. Many of the best known intellectuals of that time were Masons. The Grand Lodge, as an institution, affirmed its *non-political character*; but its members, their commitment as Masons and citizens. Grand Master Govín said it would be a *major misfortune if there were separation between Freemasonry and Citizens*, because the work of Freemasonry would be lost.

Until late 1800s, neither Cuba nor Puerto Rico had political parties, clubs, unions, or civic organizations. For, most of these institutions were forbidden by the colonial authorities, or had not yet been created. There were few schools, especially mid-level education, and one university in Havana. *Freemasons grew intellectually* by participating in the Lodges and literary societies. Freemasonry became, for most Masons, *their school*, as well as the vehicle through which they prepared themselves to become future leaders, able to undertake their patriotic endeavors.

The fundamental contribution of Freemasonry to nation-building, in Cuba and Puerto Rico was through three key functions: *the connective, the disseminating and the incubating functions.*

Autochthonous Freemasonry functioned as a true school of political and socio-economic leaders, especially for those Brethren lacking economic opportunity to obtain a formal higher education. This was the greatest contribution of Freemasonry in the Spanish Antilles."

This information may help explain the variations that some may have observed in my work. The entire paper is in: https://web.cortland.edu/romeu/AQC131.11%20Final-Romeu2018.pdf

Jorge L. Romeu

Onondaga District Mentoring Chair

The Mentoring Corner

May 2021

Hello, Brethren:

As I do every year, I drove down to Florida to visit my son and grandchildren, and to talk with my Mentor — a seasoned Mason that has occupied all the positions in the Grand Lodge of this state. He still keeps very busy, and has always given me the best advice.

Currently, my Mentor is working on regularizing some Hispanic Masonic groups, in Florida. Regular Masons come from Latin America, with little English and a different ritual. It is not easy for them to integrate into regular American Lodges. So, some create their own irregular Lodges. My Mentor is facilitating links with Spanish-speaking Lodges in South Florida, so that they can join them, or creating new Lodges with them, as well as other GL of Florida Hispanic Masons.

He then asked me what new things I was working on and how they are coming along. "Since you first told me about the *Readings*, I knew you would get into trouble with some", he said. "I know you well and understand what you are trying to do. Those who don't know you, will not". I explained that, in addition to the meaning of this work in the US, it had another implication. I am in contact with the Grand Lodge of Cuba. And I stress the relation between Mason and Citizen. I would be a big hypocrite if I asserted that approach there, and maintained another one, here.

I told him how, at the start of Castro's regime, the Grand Lodge of Cuba held a big meeting. There were two sides, and two issues. First, those who supported Castro claimed that his regime incarnated the beliefs of Freemasonry, and proposed that the Grand Lodge disband, donated its wealth to the government, and join it. Then, there were those who, like my father, claimed that our Institution was independent, and should thus remain. The latter group carried, and the Grand Lodge of Cuba, under whatever restrictions it has to live with, is still there and is still working.

We then talked about strengthening Lodge organization and cohesion. Statistically, members started declining from the 1950s on. What happened then? New media (television) and a move to the suburbs, as well as to other cities, in search of better opportunities, changed people's life.

The old system, where people lived in the same town, knew each other, and socialized in the Lodges and local organizations, started to change. In the new suburbs many people were not well acquainted with each other. New family life included evenings at home, watching TV. The social function of the Lodge started to change as new forms of socialization took over. Things became even more complex with the appearance of the Internet, email, social media, and Zoom.

Freemasonry must respond by becoming more creative, and thrive under the new conditions. We currently *advertise* in Grand Lodge's web page and get *Hits*. Candidate information is sent to local NorthStar mentors. But half of the Candidates never respond to our contact emails. And, of those who do, and actually go through the three Degrees, half leave our Institution shortly after.

Lodges need to establish a *theme*, to provide stability. We have discussed this before, in our column. In England, there are

Lodges supporting sports cars, motorcycling, etc.. We need to think about creating different themes for our Lodges: hunting, fishing, camping, canoeing, hiking, gun ownership, etc.. Such activities may attract member interest beyond the Three Degrees, and make them want to come to Lodge because, before or after the session, they can develop such interests.

Currently, candidates are linked to Lodges close to their homes. But this is not efficient, nor enough, because said Lodges may well be integrated by Brothers with different interests than those of candidates. And bonds established may well be too few, or too weak, for them to stay.

Jorge L. Romeu
Onondaga District Mentoring Chair

The Mentoring Corner

August 2021

Hello, Brethren:

During our last Lodge meeting, a dear Brother who is a Past Master and NorthStar Coach, said to me that our first and foremost function was to *make new Masons*. I had heard this concept before, and it didn't sound correct. Thence, I looked up in my Ritual the answer to: what came you here to do. It reads: to learn to subdue my passions and improve myself in Masonry!

To *subdue* means to *bring under control, especially by an exertion of the will*. Passions are intense and barely controllable emotions. Some are positive (https://designepiclife.com/things-to-be-passionate-about/) — and others (e.g., vices) not so much. These are the ones to be controlled.

Then, it states: to *improve* in Masonry. What is the definition of Freemasonry? For, we need it to define how to become a better one. What does it mean to be a Mason? What does it imply, in practice? Is Freemasonry a club? Or is it an Institution? And if it is neither, what is it then?

According to Google, a *Club* is an *association or an organization dedicated to a particular interest or activity*. On the other hand, an *Institution* is a *society or an organization founded for a religious, educational, social, or other similar purpose*. Let's analyze these two different things!

We surely are *not a Club*, for we have all these *Obligations*, *Charges*, *Rituals*, etc.. that we endorse and should follow, which go way beyond what any Club requires from its members.

Therefore, we must be an Institution, in which case, what are we founded for? A good way to find out is to re-read our Charges and Obligations. Let's review those of the First Degree:

There, we are taught that Masons uphold *three attributes: Brotherly love, relief, and truth*. The first means that we should cherish and respect each other; the second, that we should help those of us who fall into hard times; the last one, that we should pursue the search of our truth.

Then the Charge tells how there are *three great duties* which, as Masons, we should strictly observe and inculcate: *to God, to our Neighbors, and to Ourselves*. God is a higher spiritual being that represents all goodness, and we should revere; our Neighbors represent members of society at large; and to Ourselves implies that we should strive to become the very best that we can be.

Regarding Country, the Charge instructs us to be quiet and peaceable citizens, true to our government and just to our country; and *not to countenance disloyalty or rebellion*. Freemasonry does not tell us what creed, religious or civic, to believe in. Instead, it teaches us to follow the one our heart supports, but to respect and tolerate those others with which we do not agree. In these trying times, *The Craft has much to contribute, by way of example, to society in general.*

Lodge openings and closing, as well as Degree Rituals, have by objective to teach or remind us of our Institution's most important principles. We need to learn and internalize them, so we can continuously practice them. We need to talk about these concepts with new Candidates, in our Northstar courses, so they become fully aware about the kind of Institution they will join. It is especially important these days, when we are advertising Freemasonry in the Internet and in Billboards, to people that have seldom heard of us — or that have heard the wrong things about us.

Finally, we need to teach these values during the Degree Instruction sessions. This Mentor strongly believes in a deliberate Degree pace, that allows new Brothers the time to learn and to adjust. Brethren don't need to be rushed through the three Degrees. If we conduct business in the First Degree, even recently Initiated Brethren can participate in Lodge work. They can be Raised at the end of the year, having spent two or three months thoroughly learning each Degree taken.

Jorge L. Romeu
Onondaga District Mentoring Chair

The Mentoring Corner

September 2021

Hello, Brethren:

Last month, we looked up in the Ritual the answers to several interesting topics. We will continue reviewing its Entered Apprentice section, in search of more Light in Masonry.

Before entering the Lodge room, Candidates are asked several questions: that they have not requested admission to our Institution by improper solicitations, or mercenary motives, but by a favorable opinion, a desire of *knowledge*, and a wish of being of service to fellow creatures.

After taking the Obligation, the new Brother is introduced to the *Great Light*: volume of the Sacred Law, and is explained that, *howsoever men differ in creed or theology*, he can there find the principles of morality upon which to build a righteous life. He is told also that *adopting no particular creed, encouraging each one to be steadfast in the faith of his acceptance, he should direct his life by the light he should find, and as he should there find it*. For, as long as such a Light shines upon our Altars, so long can Freemasonry continue to live and *shed its beneficial influence upon mankind*. Let's examine again, these very powerful words of wisdom.

The very first thing a newly made Brother is shown, is the volume of the Sacred Law, with the admonition that *each one may adopt his own particular creed*, his faith of acceptance, and to find its Light as he would, in his own way. This is Freemasonry at its best, pure and simple.

In religion, in philosophy, in politics, Freemasonry gives you a leeway to define your own, as long as it is honest and you *respect those of others*, believing they have also been defined by honest thoughts. I do not know of any other Institution that gives its members such freedom of choice and action, paired with an obligation to afford others, with the same choice and action.

Then, the Ritual mentions obligation to our Fellow Men. We find similar statements in many parts: service to fellow creatures; to shed Freemasonry's beneficial influence upon mankind etc.. But, do we actually understand the depths of this, elusive, obligation to serve mankind?

We all serve mankind in straightforward ways: we work hard and well in our jobs, pay our taxes, raise worthy children, are good neighbors, etc.. These deeds are expected, and we fulfill our duties. But occasionally, we go above and beyond our duty: spend more time on it, prepare more, or even do things that are not part of our duties. Some of our District Lodges build ramps for the handicap, operate food pantries, run BBQs to raise funds for charities, and for children.

Some activities are small, still important; others have larger repercussions. But all of them contribute to serving our Fellow men, and to shedding Freemasonry's beneficial influence upon mankind. These activities provide the favorable opinion of the Craft, that our Ritual suggests.

As modern life has changed, so have the means of introducing Candidates to the Craft. In present days, people move often. And many loose the family and friends contacts that served to introduce them to Freemasonry. We now use websites, Internet, billboards etc., to make people aware of our existence. But we still seek Candidates that come in search of knowledge and wish to be of service to their fellow men, discarding those who come for mercenary or petty motives.

The Word published, in its three most recent issues, an account of the Morgan Affair and the Anti-Masonic movement, occurring around 1820 to 1845. We can extract several positive lessons from those experiences. In its desire to grow The Craft some flawed individuals, with mercenary intentions, were admitted. They used our Craft to promote selfish goals, business or politics. As a result, our Institution suffered two decades of withdrawals and attacks, and it almost disappeared.

Jorge L. Romeu
Onondaga District Mentoring Chair

The Mentoring Corner

October 2021

Hello, Brethren:

On September 20, about 50 NorthStar District Chairs and DDGMs attended a zoom meeting organized by RW Menegon, Chair of the NorthStar Committee. Its objective was to present the Membership Development Committee report which is essentially composed of two parts. The First, develops a number of statistics about the program, which can be synthesized as:

Website
\# Viewed   935,462
\# Visits   18,546
\# DaysTot 1,312

Totals
Cost $17,520
Cost/Click $.95
MMasons 63
Cost/MM 277.28

For example, for $17,520, over 935 thousand persons clicked on the website, leading to 63 new Master Masons, for a cost of $277.78 per Master Mason raised (the Petition fee is $175).

The Second part of the Report included two interesting digressions: about Member retention, through improved Lodge programs; and about developing stronger community presence through increased partnering with other civic groups in joint community events. Also, identifying with the Craft by wearing Masonic paraphernalia, since "every Mason performs public relations".

We espouse the concepts in the Second part of the report. We have always, from these pages as well as Lodge Master, encouraged and developed Masonic programs for our Lodge, and joint community programs that enhance broader exposure of our Craft. We also believe that Brethren demeanor in the community (as parents, neighbors, citizens, volunteers, etc.) is the best advertisement that we can provide. Words are carried away by wind; deeds remain, and speak by themselves.

We do have some differences of opinion regarding the First part because we find that results obtained, given the resources allocated, are weak. From our engineering background we learned that every course of action requires also a goal and a time line, in order to assess its outcome.

For example, we want to allocate $17K expecting to raise at least 100 new Masons in a year, given that the cost of Initiation is $175 (and 17520/175 ~100). If, at the end of the time line, the course of action falls short, then it is time to consider other alternatives. Such valuation is very important because, in the zoom meeting, it was announced that Grand Lodge will spend about

$5600 per month in NorthStar, through Ads distributed by billboards, Internet, social media, etc..

A break-even point for this second amount is: $5600/$175, ~32 new Masons/month. So, it would be useful, if only for comparison, to explore other courses of action, and their outcomes.

For example, each of our 48 districts could be given ($5600/48=) $116 to develop their own outreach programs (e.g., Lodge activities, open to the public, with a paid speaker, on some local topic of interest; or with an unpaid speaker, but offering food and refreshments for all attendees).

Or selected District Lodges can offer worthy candidates partial relief (e.g., 50% discount) in their Initiation fees. Alternatively, said money can be given to Lodges that need to improve their appearance (e.g., paint their building façades, enhance their Masonic signs, furniture, and other features that make visitors feel welcome in their premises, and encourage them to come back).

In engineering, trade-off analyses are implemented all the time, and nobody is offended by it. Its objective is to select the best course of action; one that gives the best bang for the buck!

They say that all politics is local. Similarly, Freemason recruiting is local. Remember the time you joined the Craft? Was it because you knew someone who was a Mason and impressed you positively? I joined because my father, the man I have most loved and revered, was one.

Jorge L. Romeu
Onondaga District Mentoring Chair

The Mentoring Corner

November 2021

Hello, Brethren:

One of the first things we do, when running a prospective Candidate through the NorthStar Program, is to present and discuss the *Masonic Compact*. This document defines, in an abridged way, Freemasonry. It is positive for all of us to revisit the *Compact* from time to time.

The *Compact* starts with: "Because I am a Freemason, I believe that Freedom of Religion is an inalienable human right, and tolerance an indispensable trait of human character", and affirms to "respect their beliefs as they respect mine". This can be extended beyond just religious thought.

It continues: "education and the rational use of the mind are the keys to facing the problems of humanity". And then adds: "I will bring my questions and my ideas to my Lodge". In short, Masons read, think, and exchange ideas with their brothers, in an environment of tolerance.

Then: "traditions and Ritual are important platforms for growth and learning". Adding: "the mission of the Craft to provide tools, atmosphere, challenges and motivation to help Brothers do the same". There are many moral teachings in our rituals, to be learned and put to practice. Sometimes we just go over the Ritual, without thinking through about all the things it is teaching us.

The *Compact* then talks about our Institution's social commitment: "personal community service is the best demonstration of one's commitment to humanity; I acknowledge that words without deeds are meaningless, and I vow to work with my Lodge to provide service to the community". Service would do wonders for attracting, recruiting and retaining new members.

Another very important part says: "my obligation to community extends beyond my local sphere and is partly fulfilled in my patriotism: love of my country, obedience to its laws and celebration of its freedoms", including helping to heal our divisions, through brotherly love.

It then states: "leadership is best demonstrated by commitment to serving others". Masons lead, especially by example. To be a leader does not necessarily mean standing on a soap box.

It also says: "friendship, fidelity and family are the foundations of a well-lived life" which is very clear. It continues: "the last great lesson of Freemasonry is the value of personal integrity": Masons are principled men. Finally it adds: "I therefore vow to be a man of my word".

The *Compact* ends by: "Masonry's power is best exercised when its Light is shared with the world at large". And adds: "to present myself to the world as a working Freemason, on the path to building a more perfect temple". Again, the *Compact* encourages us to become more active in our communities, and to become the best Ad that Freemasonry can have: ourselves. We have written many times in this column, that such is the best way to attract, recruit and retain new members.

The *Compact* interpretation, as that of every document, is very personal. But as upright men that we Masons are, our interpretations will probably not differ much from that of each other. The complete *Compact* can be found in: https://web.cortland.edu/romeu/MasonicCompact.pdf

Grand Lodge took place in Utica, last month. Deputy Grand Master, RW Richard Kessler, was predictably elected Grand Master. The new Deputy Grand Master election was important, as the newly elected DGM will likely become our next Grand Master in two years. There were four candidates. It ran three rounds, after which RW S. Rubin was selected. You can read more details about the Grand Lodge in our Editor's Prerogative, as well as in the four DDGM reports.

It was nice having the Grand Lodge upstate. This may have allowed a greater participation, mainly from upstate Masons, some of which may find difficult to attend GL in New York City.

Jorge L. Romeu
Onondaga District Mentoring Chair

The Mentoring Corner

December 2021

Hello, Brethren:

Last month I read an article about membership recruiting and retainment issues on American Legion and the VFW. It said that, instead of looking into why members leave we should also investigate why members stay in the organization. That is what we do in this article.

Freemasonry is a *big tent Institution*, and its members remain for many different reasons. Firstly, Fellowship: when we join a Lodge, we befriend its members. If we work with Masonic Districts, we befriend other Lodge members. If we join Appended Bodies, webefriend members from contiguous Districts. And as Fellowship is multifaceted, it may take very different forms.

If we travel and visit Lodges in other cities, we further widen our circle. In New York City, many Lodges are organized by ethnic groups: Hispanic, German, French, Italian, etc., the same as in Washington DC: Filipino, Arab, etc.. They work *in their own languages*, and provide social gatherings for family and friends living in the area. Visiting is very enlightening and enjoyable.

In other countries (e.g., England) Lodges gather Brothers with similar hobbies or avocations. There are Lodges for car, motorcycles, boating, enthusiasts. We have suggested using themes in our Lodges: fishing, hunting, canoeing, gun practices, etc., to help attract and keep members.

Another very strong reason for remaining is Ritual. We all look up to our Ritual for learning about our Craft, Lodge officers' duties, Degree particulars, as well as Freemasonry's many and excellent teachings, which help us become better men. Others are interested in Ritual procedures and improvements, For them, Observant Lodges were created by the Grand Lodge.

Others, have an interest in investigating the origins and developments of Freemasonry, both in time and across different nations. For them, GL has Research Lodges in Buffalo and in NYC.

Other Brethren have an interest in exploring social and public issues, from a non-partisan, non-political point of view. Freemasonry is a strong member of Civil Society, one that embraces important philosophical tenets (tolerance, brotherly love, and devotion to Country). Such is part of Service to Humanity. But they do not have a space to meet and exchange views. Through *The Word*, they raise some issues and bring them to the attention and consideration of other Brethren.

At the start of this difficult year, some of us, concerned with the divisions in the country and the bitterness of the debates, started reading *The Federalist Papers*, written long ago, also during troubled times. We thought these could help lower the tone of public discussion and contribute to heal and unite. Such effort was misinterpreted by some, who thought it was political: it was not!

We want to restart this effort by exploring issues that contribute to lower the tone and bridge divisions. Our Tolerance and Brotherly Love should allow us to examine, in harmony. Opening such meetings to our own communities, may help give greater exposure to The Craft, increase its membership, and provide a badly needed public example of respectful discussion of civic issues.

Those interested in joining in this effort need to meet, plan what to do, and how to go about it. In January, I will send out Zoom links for short meetings, every second and fourth Fridays of each month, at 7 pm, to work on planning. It would be helpful if the DDGMs, and the Leaders of the Appended Bodies of the four Districts covered by *The Word*, would pass said links on to their respective Lodge Masters. And that these would make them available to their Lodge Members.

By the time this issue of *The Word* comes out, we will be celebrating New Year: Festival of Lights, Hannukah, Christmas and other festivities. To all, health, happiness and peace, in 2022!

Jorge L. Romeu
Onondaga District Mentoring Chair

2022

The Mentoring Corner

January 2022

Hello, Brethren:

Following up on our article of January 2022, we want to propose a Program that can become a powerful recruiting tool: the development of zoom and community talks/meetings to help foster Civility. Freemasonry, with its known *Tolerance and Brotherly Love tenets and its obligations of Love of Country and Service to Humanity* is well positioned to contribute to this.

There are other useful activities to serve our community that Lodges are already undertaking (manning food drives and food banks, building ramps for the handicap, giving toys for Xmas and organizing egg hunts in Easter, etc.). But for Brethren interested in contributing to lower the tone of public discussions and to bridge our country's divisions, this new project is of significance.

Said project is in line with MWGM Kessler's Empire State Mason article (Winter 2021) and PGM Russ Charnovia's Excelsior

Lecture on Civility Mosaic (https://vimeo.com/661808284 [video unavailable]) at NYCOD/AASR-NMJ on XII/28/21. PGM R. Charnovia organized a group that created website http://MasonicCivility.org several years ago, to show how Freemasonry can help foster Civility.

Last year, after the riot and invasion of the US Capitol, we started a Zoom group to read *The Federalist Papers*. This year, we want to restart this effort with a different approach. Links were sent to DDGMs and Leaders of Appended Bodies of the Districts covered by *The Word*, for two short Zoom meetings, on Fridays January 14th and 28th at 7 pm, to work on planning. If all goes well, we will continue meeting monthly, every second and fourth Fridays, at 7 pm. We greatly appreciate if DDGMs pass said links to their Lodge Masters, and these, to their Lodge Members.

We want to start with a Brainstorming session to decide what to do and how to go about it. We will look at events that contribute to increase divisions in our country and the bitterness of debates, and what can Freemasonry do to help, from a non-partisan, non-political point of view.

Such task can have several forms: presenting topics with one speaker, two speakers debating, or a panel. Finding an appealing and attractive format is of importance to enhance the participation.

The Media, currently widely polarized, has a responsibility in exacerbating our divisions and toxic tone of our debates. Providing non-partisan, factual information may help improve things.

For example, much debate goes on about voting procedures, gerrymandering, filibustering, the House-Senate reconciliation process, etc.. Does everybody know and understand what these concepts involve? What were the initial objectives pursued by these measures? What alternatives are available? What are the consequences, if they are modified? Providing neutral, technical explanation and information about said concepts may help decrease the toxic level of debates.

We can start by organizing several internal group discussions, to verify that they are civil, interesting and informed. If so, we may want to open them to the public. One way to promote them is via partnering with other groups: Rotarians, Public Library, VFW, the Legion, etc.. By opening our deliberations to the public, such Project becomes an excellent Recruiting Tool. For,some of our friends and neighbors may want to attend. One thing is to listen to a Pundit talking about an issue, and another is to hear it from somebody *closer to home*. This may give our Craft more exposure, sending an important message: *Freemasons care*. By becoming more relevant and better known in our communities, we may attract new members and improve our relations.

It sounds good on paper but, *will it work?* Implement it as an engineering project: prototype first (Lodge, District). If it fulfills its goals, *learn, fix and expand. Finally, adopt and replicate.*

Jorge L. Romeu
Onondaga District Mentoring Chair

The Mentoring Corner

February 2022

Hello, Brethren:

I read with interest the extensive article, *Roman Catholicism and Freemasonry*, by Bro. Dudley Wright (Part 7), taken from *The Builder*, that our Editor published last month. It provides what I would call the macro description of the problem (that touches the highest levels). I would like to digress about some micro motives that explain how Freemasons, from places such as Cuba and Puerto Rico, where I originally come from, dealt with such issues on a daily basis.

An American friend, Irish Catholic, once asked me how I could be both Mason and Catholic. My reply was that, in Cuba and PR, most people are Catholic. You can't make Masons from any other. And we do not find problems, because we understand the origins of such disagreements.

In Spain the Catholic Church was used as a tool to support the King. Inquisition took care of dissent, religious and political. *Operative Masons vanished* when cathedrals were no longer built. There was scant middle class interested in using the Masonic structure to create the modern Craft that we know today in England. In Spain, King and Church saw such an Institution as a menace.

In England, the first Grand Lodge, created in 1717, supported the newly established House of Hanover when King George I became, in 1714, the first Hanoverian monarch. And Masons became vigorous in social and political life throughout the Eighteenth and Nineteenth Centuries.

In Spain, Freemasonry essentially entered with Napoleon's French invasion, and supported parliamentary Liberalism. The Church supported the absolute King and Conservatism. Thence, Liberals became Masons. And throughout the Nineteenth Century Freemasonry was so influential that often, Grand Master and Scottish Rite Grand Commander, were similarly the leaders of their political parties. As a result, Catholic Church and Freemasonry attacked each other, not only on the grounds of institutional values, but also on the basis of their political positions and interests.

In Cuba and PR, during the second half of the Nineteenth Century, Freemasons supported the Autonomy and an insular parliament for these colonies. The Catholic Church however, supported absolute control by Spain. Our Grand Masters were also, leaders of Autonomic political parties.

When I was growing up, in Cuba, I attended catholic school, where I was told in class by religious teachers, terrible stories about Masons. When I went home, I asked my father about it, and he straightened the record. There were religious booklets such as *Catholic and Mason?* that questioned the possibility of being both, because this was a very frequent situation. Often, in our small towns, we would find that the Judge, Mayor, doctor, pharmacist, police chief, parish priest, teacher and the leaders of the main political parties and civic organizations, were members of the Lodge, which provided them a neutral place to meet/discuss community issues, of interest to all.

In our Lodge, I have helped organize community activities such as student orientation day sand talks on topics of interest. I have found that some folks are intimidated when coming to our Lodges, especially women. They feel uncomfortable due to the sense of secrecy that still exists in the mind of some. One of the things we need to do is to *offset such feelings*, which does not help in recruiting and retainment efforts — especially coming from candidate wives and daughters.

In our January article, we proposed a new program: development of zoom and live talks and meetings, to help foster partisan Civility. Freemasonry, known for its Tolerance, Brotherly Love, and Service to Country and Humanity, is well-positioned to contribute to Civility. I set two Zoom meetings to get organized, but nobody showed up. Thence, I will drop the idea, for now.

Jorge L. Romeu
Onondaga District Mentoring Chair

The Mentoring Corner

March 2022

Hello, Brethren:

This month I would like to comment on our Editor's piece *A few words about the publishing process*, concerning our monthly newspaper *The Word*. I don't believe there are many other Masonic Districts in our Grand Lodge that have a feature as *The Word*. Our monthly newspaper keeps us informed about what happens in our four CNY Districts and Lodges, prints useful Masonic readings that can be used as instruction material (since we all receive it and there is no need to duplicate it), and it is also a generator of ideas and programs to develop or emulate.

There is much work poured into our monthly journal. First and foremost, by our Editor, who reads them and then puts all the articles together. But also, from the many contributors that write periodical articles about what is going on in our Districts, at all levels. Skimming through them, we can choose which Lodges or events to attend, and plan ahead when to attend them.

And there are, of course, *the readers*: the most important part. For it is for them that all this work is created. *The Word* publishes 3000+ copies, digital and print, distributed every month to CNY Masons. Are all us, readers, getting the most out of this excellent Masonic vehicle?

I was happy to find out how some readers did react (positively and negatively) to the article on Catholicism and Freemasonry that appeared last month. This indicates that people read *The Word* and considers its content, which is the final objective of all this collective effort!

I have done some journalism on the side (https://web.cortland.edu/romeu/articles.html) for many years. I remember how, when I first arrived in CNY over forty years ago, there was at least one independent newspaper in every town. Recall *Rome Sentinel*, *Cortland Standard* or *Syracuse Herald*, to name a few. CNY people wrote for them. Today, most – if not all – of them have all but disappeared. This is a nation-wide situation. Its importance lies in the fact that such independent newspapers are channels that debate new thoughts and opinion. Had we still such independent media in every town, we would perhaps have less acrimony in our national conversations.

Another event of importance, these days, is the war that is taking place in Ukraine. Grand Lodge has made contact with its Ukrainian counterpart, and will send money to help relieve the suffering of that population, who is living through daily bombardments and battles. Other Grand Lodges are also contributing money to help mitigate the Ukrainian distress.

I can empathize with those hurting there as I was a 17-year-old high school student living in Havana, during the Cuban Missile Crisis, in October 1962. President Kennedy told Mr. Khrushchev to get his missiles out, or else. Mr. Castro was not happy with such decision, for he was left out of the negotiations. But a disastrous war, which could have brought to us in Cuba, the terrible fate that Ukrainians are now undergoing, was averted. Let's pray this calamity is resolved soon.

Finally, an interesting new effort is under development by Grand Lodge. On February 9th, our Deputy Grand Master, Bro. Steven Rubin, sent out a letter in which he invited all to "help man our committees, sub-committees and Boards" and "find real solutions to the challenges that we continue to face in our Lodges and our Districts". Their final objective is to "help shape the face and future of New York Masonry". DGM Rubin is asking us to contribute with our personal skills such as "leadership, management, or professional experience or talent, and a desire to work with Brothers across New York State". The letter provides a website, where interested Brethren can submit their information. This seems to be an appropriate endeavor to help undertake.

Jorge L. Romeu
Onondaga District Mentoring Chair

The Mentoring Corner

April 2022

Hello, Brethren:

Last month we went for a full week to Washington DC, to babysit our grandson. As I always do when I am in DC during the week, I visited the Scottish Rite Library in the House of the Temple (HOT). There, its helpful librarian Ms. Larissa W., showed me some material that retiring scholar Ill. Brent Morris had donated. I read the article, *Notes on Teaching The Craft* (https://web.cortland.edu/romeu/Notes%20on%20teaching%20the%20craft.pdf in the Scottish Rite Journal. It described a singular example of an unorthodox seminar for College students.

We do need to explain what The Craft is and what it stands for, to people outside it. My own experience is that many are afraid of, or do not like, our Institution. I have noticed how some are concerned about entering our Lodges, when we open them for public activities. And I have tried, without success, to give seminars in the colleges I worked because some administrators saw them as disquieting. Only once, thanks to a personal friend and colleague, I gave a talk about the 300th Anniversary of The Craft (https://web.cortland.edu/romeu/SandSeminarMason2017.pdf).

The course taught by Dr. and Br. Jose Diaz, at Ohio State University, explaining to a young audience what we are, is such an important event. As Sean Connery said to Mr. Nash (Costner) in *The Untouchables*, referring to where to recruit good candidates: *we need to go to the tree and not the pile*. We need to concentrate in letting young people know that we don't bite or have tails or horns, nor want to overthrow the government. We are good neighbors, trying to become better men, working in projects that help improve environments and communities. When *profanes* are convinced of this, then some of them may want to join Freemasons and become part of our work.

Br. Jose Diaz teaching method worked very nicely. He started by asking students what they knew about Freemasonry: all sorts of nonsense came up. He did not counter these; he let students find the answers by themselves throughout the course. Br. Diaz used two approaches: not to turn the course into a recruiting tool, and not to use material based on undocumented, tradition-based Freemasonry writings, but fact-based, historical material, of which there is much out there.

In the past fifty years, there has been much serious scholarship written about Freemasonry, that we can use to make our case. Some has been written by Freemasons who, as Bro. Diaz, are scholars themselves. Bro. Mark Tabbert (https://www.linkedin.com/in/mark-tabbert-1908615/) is one: he has a good and well-researched history of American Freemasonry. And, of course, the Quatour Coronati Masonc Lodge (https://www.quatuorcoronati.com/). We find many sources in the British Columbia Grand Lodge site (https://freemasonry.bcy.ca/texts/index.html).

There are several academic associations such as REHMLAC (https://revistas.ucr.ac.cr/index.php/rehmlac) and CEHME (https://cehme.com/), two serious Spanish language research sources.

Grand Lodge offers, through its Livingston Library, interesting Freemasonry talks for New York City residents: https://www.youtube.com/channel/UCzwVcQe9QmE_KJ7nQiBiGLA. But, for audiences outside that area, open Zoom illustrative talks or presentations could be organized and advertised, using Br. Diaz approach of *not to turn them into a recruiting tool, and not to use material based on undocumented, tradition-based Freemasonry material.*

We need to make our case: (1) combat the image that some still have about Freemasonry being a secret, suspicious society, (2) but to the contrary, we are an Institution of men of good will, who work to improve ourselves, as well as the community where we live and interact.

Jorge L. Romeu
Onondaga District Mentoring Chair

The Mentoring Corner
May 2022

Hello, Brethren:

Last month's column mentioned how we needed to explain what The Craft is and what it stands for, to people unfamiliar with it. We need to combat the false image that some still have about Freemasonry being a secret, mistrustful society, by showing them that we are an Institution of men of good will, who work hard to improve ourselves as well as the community where we live and interact. My own experience is that some persons are concerned or afraid about entering our Lodges, when we open them for public activities. And this attitude seriously hurts our recruiting and retaining efforts.

Such reaction may partially stem from the information people read and hear in the Media, that often either ignores Freemasonry at all, or misrepresents its tenets. I will give below two recent examples.

Last month, PBS aired an excellent TV documentary about Bro. Benjamin Franklin, who was an extraordinary man in many ways, and served his country and his fellow citizens well. Bro. Franklin was not only a Mason, but a Grand Master of the Grand Lodge of Pennsylvania. However, not one word about his membership in Freemasonry was stated in said TV documentary, which ran for four hours.

On May 2nd, a large national newspaper published a long review of the book "First in the Hearts of His Brethren", about Bro. George Washington's membership in The Craft. The books was written by Bro. Mark Tabbert, a seasoned Masonic scholar and Washington Masonic Memorial curator, Alexandria VA.

The first part of said article is a standard book review. But in the second part, the author embarks in a series of inaccurate commentaries, possibly stemming from a lack of understanding of our Institution. So, I wrote a letter to the Editor providing some corrections. I will present several such corrections, below.

The author states that "Masonic practice mirrors and parallels religious rites". Masonic rituals are not religious: *Freemasonry is a system of morality veiled in allegory, illustrated by symbols.* We Masons are religious (belief in a Supreme Being and in afterlife, is a requirement), but Freemasonry is not a religion. The author adds: "membership in the Masons is forbidden by the Catholic Church". That was many years ago, but it's no longer true. The Catholic Church does not encourage its members to join Freemasonry — but accepts it. I am a practicing Catholic, like thousands of other Latin American and American Masons.

The author then objects about we "claiming [our] organization is the repository of ancient secrets of Solomon's temple". We use tradition to enrich ritual. But Freemasonry is much more than that. Modern (speculative, as opposed to operative) Craft was created at the beginning of the XVIII Century. Then, the world was ruled by autocratic monarchs and severe churches, and its society was strictly divided into classes. *The Craft revolutionized its time by stating that, in Lodge, all Masons are equal; by establishing elections to select our leaders, and by requiring tolerance and respect for the ideas of others.*

The author states "the need for more extensive scholarship" regarding Freemasonry and its members. Apparently, the author ignores how such serious academic scholarship has existed for over half a century, and we have given examples of it in our Mentor column of last month. Finally, the author states how "a torrent of sensational conspiracism inundates the public" — much of it acquired from the Media itself.

Let's do some numbers: NY state has about 18 million citizens. Half are women and, of the men, half are too young/old to be Masons, are felons, ill, etc.. This leaves 4.5 million *potential Masons*. There are about 30 thousand New York Masons, yielding a ratio of 0.00667 or 6.67 Masons per thousand apt New Yorkers. Said newspaper has a daily circulation of 75,0000 copies. Assuming half its readership are men, multiplying it by 0.00667, we get 2500 potential Mason readers. If only 1% of such readers would have sent a letter to the Editor, as I did, commenting the mentioned book review, about 25 letters would have been received by the newspaper Editor. So far, no letter has been published regarding said review article.

We need to counter Media misinformation with larger community participation, and by opening our Lodges to public events. People are smart enough, and will see for themselves who we really are.

Jorge L. Romeu
Onondaga District Mentoring Chair

The Mentoring Corner
August 2022

Hello, Brethren:
This is not our first column dedicated to talk about the importance of MWD (Masters, Wardens and Deacons) Meetings, which unfortunately are no longer taking place. We will provide here

some additional elements that stress the value of preserving the MWDs.

Freemasonry is a social activity. I am a member of a Puerto Rican Lodge. I could seldom visit, so I joined the Liverpool Lodge. Then, I felt a need to meet District Brothers from other Lodges. I joined the DDGM's *family*, visiting all District Lodges, and participating in MWD Bimonthly Meetings, where I met and befriended many Brothers more. I then joined the Scottish Rite, where I befriended even more Brethren, from Masonic Districts adjacent to Onondaga.

My objective was much more than just social. The interaction with so many Brothers helped me grow Masonically and provided many new ideas, some of which I have aired in this column.

Associations have at least two values: first, to fulfill the purpose for which they were created; then to put people in contact. MWD's were created to help District Lodges coordinate their work and instruct leaders about issues of importance and concern to our Institution. Collaborating and exchanging views and information with others expands old ideas, fosters new ones and develops efficient ways to enhance joint programs. These are, possibly, MWDs most powerful functions.

Currently, our country is extensively divided on several central issues. The level of discord has become toxic. The Media is similarly divided into partisan lines; audiences join those outlets that reinforce their views. Organizations, where both sides of an issue are examined with balance and moderation, are rare. Partisan deliberations of commentators and analysts exacerbate things.

We believe Freemasonry can contribute *two key components* to help diffuse tension. First, it can *provide information* about the topics in question. Secondly, and perhaps more important yet, to examine them in a *Tolerant atmosphere*, showing that one can respectfully and fairly disagree on any subject. In these difficult times, this would be a great contribution to reduce friction.

Let's provide an illustrative example: *the voting system controversy*. What is it? What does it pursue? What are its limitations? What alternative voting systems are there? Many *discrepancies stem from a lack of basic understanding or of knowledge*, of key facts involved in the problem.

This Mentor, as some readers may have noticed, strives to *fulfill Love of Country and Service to Humanity* obligations, while keeping Freemasonry's rule *not to conduct partisan politics*. We believe that such can be achieved by carefully examining challenging elements of a conflicting issue, that often create tension among the contenders, *without taking sides* in the dispute.

For example, we can organize a panel with two Brothers that support one point of view, and two that support another one, plus a Moderator. Then we open the debate to the public. To attain success, the project needs Brothers from different District Lodges to help with event attendance and advertisement. Said project would first need to be discussed and planned in the MWDs.

What would Freemasonry gain from all this? People would notice our efforts to help lower the toxic levels of partisan disagreements, thus gaining in public appreciation for our labors.

Such approach is not new to Freemasonry. For example, the Grand Lodge of Cuba stated, in 1936, also during a very heated political period, the following opinion: Freemasonry does not intend to stop the struggle between ideologies, but to *help create a climate* where everyone can defend his principles using *reason*, and achieve success based upon the *merits* of his ideas.

Jorge L. Romeu
Onondaga District Mentoring Chair

The Mentoring Corner

September 2022

Hello, Brethren:

This time, I would like to speak about the importance of *Masonic Journalism*. Like any other form of journalism, ours has at least a *double purpose*: to *inform* Brethren about what is going on (in journalism jargon, the *News section*) and to *convey ideas and evaluation*, for Brethren to think about and discuss (in journalism jargon, the *Editorial section*).

There is yet another, longer-term dimension, that is used by historians and analysts to grasp what was happening in another epoch, and how people reacted to it. For Masonic historians, this is of utmost importance. For, once we are all gone, one way to find out what was really going on, is to consult the publications of said days: Lodge records and memoirs, and the Masonic press.

Our Editor, among his important tasks, selects and publishes old articles from *The Builder*, a Masonic journal (The Builder archives (upenn.edu) published by the Masonic Research Society from 1915 until 1930. *The Builder's* information helps us gain a better knowledge of our ancient Craft. For, instruction is yet another important dimension of Masonic (and all other) journalism.

We Freemasons of Central New York, are very fortunate to possess a Masonic newspaper (I don't think many other Masonic Districts, or Grand Lodges, have one). Its existence requires, in addition to a thorough Editor, also a reliable section of contributors of news and of articles, and a loyal readership that, by perusing the newspaper, justifies the work that its laborers dedicate.

Newspapers also need funds to get published — provided to *The Word* by EMESBE and reader fees. For example, the Grand Lodge of Puerto Rico's *ACACIA* magazine is published only when there is money: not too often. Because of the scarcity of said key elements (editors, contributors, readers and funds) there are today fewer Masonic and general publications than there were, say, 50 years ago. Such a void has not been filled by social media. The need to fill it is there, and The Craft, as an important element of Civil Society, has a great opportunity to partake in this task.

We pose below some questions to our brothers, to help self-assess *The Word's* impact on us:

Do we read the general news section, in the front page? Do we read news of our own Lodge and Appended Bodies (if we belong to one)? Do we also read other Lodge news, in our own, or in neighboring Districts, to find activities that we may participate in? Do we read the reproduced articles and our *Editor's Prerogative*? Do Lodges share, or bring to its brethren attention, news or articles published in *The Word*? Is *The Word* material discussed, positively or negatively by its readers, via letters written to its Editor? Do we convey to him, comments or suggestions?

Maybe we can develop a discussion group, using Zoom, to read and analyze material that has appeared here. For example, in the front page of *The Word's* May issue, there is an excellent article titled *A Program of Masonic Service* (*The Builder*, January 1922). A century ago, Grand Lodge of North Dakota suggested to bring to the Craft in a concrete way the, means by which we Masons, individually and collectively, could serve their fellow men. Said article discussed and developed nine ways in which Masons can contribute to improve their community and country.

Is this article still valid today? If not, why not? What changes should the article require to make it valid today? How has our Craft changed, if at all, in one Century? And, if so, how?

There is enough material above to get such group started. The advantage of a Zoom instead of a Lodge meeting, is that brothers dispersed amongst Lodges, may participate, thus achieving the critical mass that makes the existence of said group viable, and also increase its attendance.

Jorge L. Romeu
Onondaga District Mentoring Chair

The Mentoring Corner

October 2022

Hello, Brethren:

On October 3rd, I gave a talk about the differences between York and Scottish rituals, as performed by the Grand Lodges of New York (USA), and of Cuba and Puerto Rico (Spanish Caribbean), in my Mother Lodge Liverpool-Syracuse No. 501. Below is a short summary.

In general, I find that there are *two types of differences* between the manner Freemasonry is observed in the United States and in Latin America (and in some parts of continental Europe).

The first type is *procedural*: that is the way ritual is done, and the way Lodges are organized.

According to the York ritual, Lodges have blue walls, curtains, etc.; the columns lie in front of the Inner Door, ashlars lie in the

East; there are two Masters of Ceremony, two Stewards, and one Chaplain. Until recently, Lodges mostly worked in Third Degree (now, they work in First).

According to the Scottish ritual, Lodge officers differ in the number and functions of their officers: no Chaplain, Marshall or Stewards exist, and there is only one Master of Ceremonies. But there is an Almoner, an Orator, an Expert, and two Tilers (one inside, and another outside the Lodge door). These officers' functions are both very different from ours, and very important in Lodge work. The Orator does the Invocation, greets Visitors, and is the last officer to speak, closing Lodge discussions. The Almoner collects money from the attendees, at the end of Lodge meetings. The Master of Ceremonies attends to the Altar and conducts candidates. The Expert is consulted in ritual matters, and conducts candidates. Columns stand between West and the Altar.

The second type concerns the *social connotations of Freemasonry* and stems from the epoch and circumstances of their establishment and their specific environment. American Lodges came from England in mid XVIII Century. In early XIX Century, American Freemasonry was affected by the Morgan Affair and the Anti-Masonic political movement. In addition, American society had public and private organizations that provided for social and political needs. Freemasonry took a low-key public development, concentrating in charity work and character improvement.

In the Spanish Caribbean, Freemasonry came from the US in the 1860s, when both Cuba and Puerto Rico were struggling to obtain self-government, similar to that of Canada. Lodges became centers of reunion of many domestic leaders, that discussed and planned for obtaining a peaceful evolution.

Newspapers, political parties and unions were organized and created by said Masonic leaders. Spanish authorities considered and fought domestic Freemasonry as an adversary group.

After Spain was gone, many public services were deficient, insufficient or absent. Few civil society organizations, or Lions, Rotary and Kiwanis clubs existed. Thence, Masonic Lodges took upon themselves to help create schools and libraries, fund youth sports clubs, donate supplies to poor students, etc.. Many men, who did not want to get into politics for ethical reasons (or for job related, as judges and the military were not allowed to belong to political parties) channeled their social initiatives through Masonic Lodges. Talks and seminars about family, budget, and small business planning, or public health, among many topics, were offered at Masonic Lodges. Such seminars were not partisan, but politically neutral. Their contents were rather of a policy nature, which allowed Masons of all political persuasions to participate and contribute. Such activities gave Freemasonry an excellent public reputation, and encouraged many good men to join it.

If interested, see PPT in: https://web.cortland.edu/romeu/ContrastingRituals2022.pdf. If your Lodge would like a presentation, let me know. Freemasonry practices could be a discussion topic.

Jorge L. Romeu
Onondaga District Mentoring Chair

The Mentoring Corner

November 2022

Hello, Brethren:

At the time of writing this column I am getting ready to vote in our Mid-Terms. I am worried, as I observe fewer lawn signs than in previous years. Are people losing interest, or just turning inward? For, people are being flooded with inaccurate and incomplete information.

Take political polls, for example. Polls should be impartial, and in many cases, they are not. Media and political pundits often omit key technical information: this hinders their validity. For example, *FiveThirtyEight* and *Real Clear Politics*, report election races with differences of one, two, or three percentage points, without mentioning the sampling error, which is typically greater than 3%. When differences are smaller, said races are tied. Saying one of the candidates is ahead does not help to strengthen faith in our elections, and may discourage people to vote. Sampling frames (lists of potential survey takers) are incomplete, because not all cell phones are listed. Caller IDs let users avoid answering polls. Criticism of parties, or apocalyptic statements about election results, may influence some interviewees to hold or disguise their true opinions.

Some political campaigns stress more the defects of their opponents than issues at hand. There are few debates, and those that occur, deal more with personalities than facts. Some voters do not trust the new balloting methods, introduced during the Pandemic to decrease crowds and reduce the spread of Covid, because they do not fully understand them. Candidates consider their opponents as enemies, rather than as political contenders with different ideas. The Media, which has become partisan, makes millions in advertising from politicians and political parties. None of the above issues help reduce the toxic and divisive levels the current political debate has reached.

Last month, I sent out an email to Masters of Onondaga Loges and to the District Offices covered by *The Word*, asking them to pass it on. I wanted to organize a Zoom presentation about statistics and polls, with a double intention. First, to inform on the use and validity of polls. And secondly to let our friends and neighbors know that we Masons do care about community affairs.

Also, the above issues may have an impact on post-election events. Some voters may be convinced, contrasting pre-electoral poll results and their media and pundit interpretations, that election outcomes are inconsistent with true results. This may increase yet more the mistrust that some voters already have, regarding the validity of the process, and raise the toxic levels more.

Some may ask: what relation, if any, does all the above have with Freemasonry? As an important part of Civil Society (churches, clubs, VFW, Legion, Rotary, Lions, etc.) the Craft has an interest in the political life of our country. Our obligations of Love of Country and Service to Humanity, and our proverbial tolerance and brotherly love, makes Freemasonry exceptionally suited to help our fellow citizens better understand some unclear or unsound concepts. Providing missing information and clarifying existing ones, may help to reduce toxic levels, allowing *The Craft* an opportunity to serve our country and community. We may seriously want to consider it.

Some may say that all of this is meddling into politics and that Masons should keep away from it. Politics would be to support one candidate, or criticize another. We include Independent, Republicans and Democrats. To explain and inform the public, encouraging debate on issues, and by providing a tolerant environment to do so is policy, something within Freemasonry's purview.

Maybe the time has come for those interested in examining this approach to have a Zoom meeting, and talk more about it. Those of you interested, please feel free to contact me by email.

Jorge L. Romeu
Onondaga District Mentoring Chair

The Mentoring Corner

December 2022

Hello, Brethren:

When you read this column, we will be watching the World Cup, and getting ready for the new 2023, hopefully better than the two previous years, as we are surpassing COVID and life is again starting to become as usual. But there are always some issues: there is a war going on in Europe, we have inflation, and the weather seems to be somewhat mixed up. Compared with the problems of others, these issues are unimportant, and we thank the Almighty for our good luck!

Masons are encouraged to be well-informed and inquisitive, which leads some to explore a variety of sources, analyzing their content carefully. Industrial Engineers use a simple but useful method to analyze a situation and get to the bottom of it. Said method, leading to the root-cause of the problem is known as the *Five Whys*. Let's explain how it works through an example.

Assume you are the Director of a Hospital, and someone comes to your office saying that a nurse has fallen in the third floor, and has broken her leg. You want to get to the bottom of it.

So, you go up there and ask: Why (1) did the nurse fall? Because there was some slippery liquid on the floor! Why (2) was there slippery liquid on the floor? Because on the adjoining wall there is a leaky fire extinguisher! Why (3) is said fire extinguisher leaky? Because the extinguisher seals have become hard, and they let the fluid leak! Why (4) have the extinguisher seals become hard, and leak? Because they have not been changed, as they should have! Why (5) have the seals not been changed, as they should have? Because this hospital has no maintenance procedures!

We have arrived to the root-cause of the problem: we need to create a maintenance program! Had we only wiped the original liquid from the floor, or removed that specific extinguisher, the problem could have occurred again, with another extinguisher, in another floor. The method to solve a problem requires us to first determine the root-cause, and then to provide a remedy for it.

We can use the above method, for example, to analyze why Brethren skip Lodge meetings, why Lodges do not pay their dues for The Word, or why our membership is dwindling. We can also use it to analyze general issues like: why some voters have lost faith in the electoral process, why is there so much disagreement in the nation or why do media and pundits stir public debates.

Recently we learned that our Deputy Grand Master has looked into our monthly, *The Word*, and is thinking of using it as a model for Masonic publications in other GLNY Masonic Districts. Our publication sets our CNY Masonic Districts apart, as innovative. We have a newspaper that informs of our activities, discusses new ideas, and provides Masonic education and knowledge.

For example, *The Word* December issue included a biography of Bro. Albert Mackey, a very prominent Mason, who was a renowned lecturer, edited several Masonic publications, and wrote the "History of Freemasonry" and the "Encyclopedia of Freemasonry". We believe Bro. Mackey's two main contributions were recruiting into the Scottish Rite Bro. Albert Pike, an outstanding leader and organizer who wrote Morals and Dogma (a fundamental treatise for the study of Scottish Rite philosophy and ritual), and then both working together, as Supreme Council Grand Secretary and Sovereign Grand Commander, respectively, to take the Rite to significant heights.

Another Mason of crucial importance was Joseph Fort Newton, who wrote "The Builders", and edited the magazine *The Builders*, from 1915 to 1930. We may also read an article on him, here.

Masonic writings are useful because they are read by many and their impact lasts throughout time. Such is the value of the written word! The Word needs to continue receiving our support!

Jorge L. Romeu
Onondaga District Mentoring Chair

2023

The Mentoring Corner

January 2023

Hello, Brethren:

Since the very beginning, humans were gregarious. First, they grouped in caves, where men cooperated in hunting and protecting the group, and women, in keeping the fire and rearing the children. They realized that, *jointly, they could achieve more than individually*. Thence, they formed larger groups, linked by blood: the clans; then tribes, and finally nations and empires.

Modern Freemasonry was similarly organized. During 1600s, the first English *speculative masons* were admitted into *operative lodges*. Early in the 1700s, four of such Lodges decided to unite, thus creating the first Grand Lodge, from which most other Grand Lodges originate.

In the United States, one Grand Lodge was created in each of its 50 states (plus one in DC). Then, their Grand Masters decided to create the Conference of Grand Masters of Masons in

North America, COGMNA, whose main purpose, according to its web page and to MW Jorge Aladro, Brother and friend, is to share programs and reports during its annual conference. These can be found in https://www.cogmna.info/publications/ [page unavailable]. Said web page explains COGMNA thus:

> Currently, the Conference membership consists of the Grand Lodges of the Provinces of Canada; the States of the United States of America, including the District of Columbia and Puerto Rico; the State of York, Mexico; and the American-Canadian Grand Lodge of Germany. These Grand Masters represent some 2 million Freemasons in North America. Grand Masters from countries throughout the world also attend the annual Conference to join in fellowship. The COGMNA annual Conference is the largest gathering of Grand Masters in the world.

The Conference's most important feature is that said Grand Masters share ideas about the agendas they have implemented, dealing with real-life, current situations. However, each Grand Lodge retains its independence, as the Conference does not generate obligations upon any of its participating members. COGMNA website also includes links to several masonic organization web pages: MSA (Masonic Service Assn.), Children's Foundation, Masonic Renewal, George Washington National. Memorial, Committee on Information on Recognition, and Committee of Grand Secretaries. These groups report on their work, during COGMNA's annual conference.

The 2021 Conference Welcome Address was given by MW Chris Coffman, Grand Master of the GL of Washington. It included the following passage about our current national attitude:

> "We, as Masons, have a duty, not an obligation, to teach civility. We do not have to agree, to be Brothers. Masonry needs to push the values of family, honesty, respect, tolerance and love. I believe that the world would be a much better place if we take that step and teach those who have opposing points of view to listen to each other and try to find some common ground."

At District level, we Masons can also gather to discuss common problems, find solutions of interest, and strengthen relations among Lodge leadership. We do have such an organization: the Masters, Wardens and Deacons Association, that used to meet at least quarterly, but hasn't done so since the start of the Covid Pandemic. It might prove a positive thing to revive the MWD, as it strengthens links among Lodge leaders through increasing personal bonds between them, and by broadening, improving and fostering new ideas that can then be implemented by Lodges, as well as by cooperating Districts. Existing ties can be enhanced further through MWDs meetings that include several Districts, creating the opportunity for launching new programs, whose material and personnel requirements go beyond the capabilities of a single Lodge, or even one District.

Jorge L. Romeu
Onondaga District Mentoring Chair

The Mentoring Corner
February 2023

Hello, Brethren:

Last month we wrote about the Conference of Grand Masters of Masons in North America, COGMNA. We said that the Grand Masters of the 50 American Grand Lodges formed this group because they realized that, *jointly, they could achieve more than individually*.

And we said that, at District level, we had a comparable organization: the Masters, Wardens and Deacons (MWD) Association, that used to meet periodically. But it hadn't done so since the start of the Covid Pandemic. We said MWD strengthens links among Lodge leaders, increasing personal bonds and broadening, improving and fostering new ideas that can then be executed by several cooperating Lodges and Districts. For, some times, material and personnel requirements for their implementation can go beyond the capabilities of a single Lodge, or a single District.

The good news is that, on January 31st, MWDs had a Zoom meeting, called by our DDGM Dan Campis, with the objective of resuscitating this organization. It had representations of 11 of the 12 District Lodges. Wor. Bro. Gary Campbell presented material about Leadership; and I said a few words about the benefits of Lodge leaders working together toward common goals. Then, the Masters presented themselves, and DDGM Campis updated us about the state of the district.

One issue that came up repeatedly, was the low attendance to Lodge meetings: usually 10 or 12 members. This is not good for recruitment or retainment. And one way to deal with this is to have regular joint meetings of several Lodges. This would increase attendance to much stronger numbers. Liverpool WM Rainer suggested to consider merging weaker Lodges, too. This would also help decrease operating expenses. We can always grow back when the numbers justify it.

Another issue to consider in future MWDs meetings is organizing public events, open to the community, jointly with other Lodges and local organizations such as the VFW, Legion, Rotary, Lions, Public Library, etc.. Holding public events would give us a greater visibility among our neighbors, providing the Craft with one of the finest recruiting and retention tools available.

In addition, topics for such public events could be selected to contribute to lower the toxic levels currently existing in our country. The Craft promotes brotherly love and tolerance. Thus, elaborating delicate issues in a respectful and urbane manner, would provide positive examples of civilized behavior, as well as a more balanced examination of the issues: two positive results.

We now return to last month's topic: *Conference of Grand Masters*. One of its most relevant activities is done through the Commission on Information for Recognition, that sets Standards or guidelines used to evaluate the regularity of a Grand Lodge, and determine whether it is worthy of recognition by COGMNA Grand Lodges. The Commission serves in investigative and advisory capacity, using the following criteria: Legitimacy of the origin; Exclusive territorial jurisdiction, except by mutual consent and/or treaty; and Adherence to the Ancient Landmarks, specifically, a Belief in God, use of the Volume of the Sacred Law as an indispensable part of the Furniture of the Lodge, and the prohibition of the discussion of politics and religion. MW Jorge Aladro, PGM of Florida, has been elected as the current Chair of the Commission on Information.

Some examples of reasons for not meeting these standards are: Grand Lodges disputing the same territory, or invading territory of neighboring Grand Lodges. Thence, the Grand Lodges of Ecuador, Georgia, Mozambique and Tahiti were found not to fulfill the requirements to enter in Amity with Lodges that constitute the Conference of Grand Masters of Masons in North America.

Jorge L. Romeu
Onondaga District Mentoring Chair

The Mentoring Corner
March 2023

Hello, Brethren:

Last month we wrote about the Conference of Grand Masters of Masons in North America, COGMNA, and about our own Masters, Wardens and Deacons MWD organization. This time, I would like to write something about the CIM, the Confederation of Inter-American Masons, a regional Masonic organization of The Americas (https://www.cmi1947.org/).

CMI was created in 1947, and includes 94 Masonic Obediences and Grand Lodges from 26 nations from North, South, and Central America, the Caribbean, and several European countries that had colonies in America, or that had, like Italy, a very strong immigration to the Americas. With almost half a million Masons, the CMI seeks to better understand and enrich the world in which it functions, through an exchange of ideas, activities, and experiences among its members.

CMI is divided into six "zones", containing related countries. *Zone One*, North America and Italy, includes the Grand Lodges of all Mexican states (Mexico, like Brazil and Colombia, have a federal system, just like we have in the US, where all their Grand Lodges are independent, within each state). Zone One also includes three American Grand Lodges: those of DC (the District of Columbia), New York, and New Jersey. Thence, we New York Masons, also belong to the CMI!

Zone Two comprises the Caribbean (Cuba, Dominican Republic, Haiti, and Puerto Rico) and France. *Zone Three* includes all the countries in Central America. *Zone Four*, includes the states of Colombia, plus Venezuela and Ecuador. When they became independent, in 1825, these three countries were a single nation, under the name Republic of Gran Colombia. *Zone Five* includes all the Grand Lodges of the Brazilian states. *Zone Six* includes the remaining six Latin American countries (Argentina, Chile, Peru, Uruguay, Paraguay, and Bolivia), plus Spain and Portugal.

CMI has an Executive Council, elected by its members. Its President is the Grand Master of the Grand Lodge of Peru. Each Zone has a Vice President. Past Grand Master William Sardone, of New York, is Vice President for Zone One. We find several pictures of the CMI leadership, visiting MW Sardone in our Grand Lodge, in https://www.cmi1947.org/2023/02/01/secretario-ejecutivo-presente-en-zona-1-de-la-cmi/?lang=es in January of this year.

An interesting CMI feature is its virtual (https://www.cmi1947.org/biblioteca/?lang=es) library. Its content, of free access, is divided into "folders" such as Academic, Classic, History, etc.. When we move into one of these folders, we find its material classified by languages. For example, in the folder History, for the English language, we find a document we can download https://drive.google.com/drive/folders/1oZOUKM8pBH29sxIq_TRGWxFFksqmpIin which is about the history of Freemasonry in the State of New York, dated from 1899.

We do not know of any other Masonic organization such as the CMI, for Europe or other parts of the world, which would be very useful. For example, Grand Master Kessler has created an account to donate money for the relief of victims of the recent earthquake in Turkey. Were there an organization like CMI in the Middle East, aid could be distributed more efficiently.

For example, in Puerto Rico, Masonic Lodges are ubiquitous all over the island. During Hurricane Maria, in 2017, communications with many small towns in the country side were severed. The government facilitated ham radios to the seventy Lodges in the island, who could transmit and inform back about the pressing needs, such as the lack of water, food, medicines, power, etc., that the population was suffering, which could then be flown in by helicopter.

Jorge L. Romeu
Onondaga District Mentoring Chair

The Mentoring Corner

April 2023

Hello, Brethren:

The Rose Croix Chapter of the Scottish Rite yearly keeps the *Feast of the Paschal Lamb*, a ceremony held around Holy Thursday, to remember Brethren that have passed during the year. Widows, relatives and friends, are invited. It is based on the Jewish Passover and the Christian Last Supper, but it is not a proxy for either. Said ceremony also highlights some of our Institution's main tenets.

Chapter officers, sitting around a table, have a symbolic meal of bread and wine. Candles, placed in front of each officer, are sequentially extinguished, and then rekindled by them, symbolizing the loss and the recovery of several, very important, Masonic principles. We offer them here, as "food for thought".

At the sequential extinguishing of the lights, the Master of Ceremonies (MOC) says: *God sent those to teach men the truth and free them from ignorance.*

The Secretary says: *teach them that men are children of one loving Father.*

Then, the Captain of the Guard (COG) says: *teach them that men are free and equal in His sight.*

The Orator says: *endeavor to set Truth in the place of error, Love in the place of hatred.*

The Junior Warden says: *teach mankind the truth of science and philosophy, and knowledge of Him.* The Senior Warden says: *seek to liberate tolling humanity and restore the light of free thought and free conscience.*

And the Most Wise Master says: *those who taught freedom, brotherhood, equality, truth, science, philosophy and liberty have thus received their reward.* The symbol of all is Jesus of Nazareth: teacher of faith, hope and love. The extinguishing of the lights is ended, and the room remains in a semi-darkness.

Then, music is played to mark the passage of time, and all six lights are again sequentially rekindled.

The Most Worshipful Master (MWM) then says: *the lights of Truth, Brotherhood, Equality, Liberty and Freedom may have been extinguished by intolerance and ruthless power, yet with Faith, Hope and Charity, the New Law of Love will rekindle them.*

The MOC then says: *keep sound wisdom and discretion.* After saying this, the MOC relights his candle, adding: So, may the Light of Wisdom illumine our world.

The Secretary then says: *maintain fellowship, freedom from deceit and falsehood, mutual respect for honor, confidence in a brother's integrity: "Ye shall know the truth and the truth shall make you free". So may the Light of Truth illumine our world.* Then, the COG says: Toleration: *the will to understand and respect the opinion of others. No man is infallible and the sole possessor of the truth. A Freemason grants to every man those rights which he claims for himself. So may the Light of Toleration illumine our world.*

The Orator then says: *"faith is the substance of things hoped for, the evidence of things not seen". We must have faith in God, faith in our fellowmen, faith in ourselves. So may the Light of Faith illumine our world.*

The JW says: *"Hope in action is charity, and beauty in action is goodness". Seek righteousness because it is right, justice because it is just, goodness because it is good, and truth because it is true. So may the Light of Hope illumine our world.*

The SW says: *"A new commandment I give unto you, that you love one another as I have loved you". Love's hope and Love's dream are of a world-wide Brotherhood of Man under the Fatherhood of God. So may the New Law of Love illumine our world.*

Finally, the MWM ends the Feast of the Paschal Lamb ceremony by saying: *may we commit ourselves anew to the high task of building a nobler world of freedom and justice for God and humanity.*

So may the Light that never fails, the Love that never forgets, and the Life that never ends, illumine our world.

These are, in a nutshell, several of the most important concepts that The Craft stands upon. The Feast of the Paschal Lamb, as every other Masonic ceremony, teaches and reminds us, of said crucial concepts.

Jorge L. Romeu
Onondaga District Mentoring Chair

The Mentoring Corner

May 2023

Hello, Brethren:

For the past six months I have been working on two articles in Spanish, about history of Freemasonry in the Spanish Antilles (Cuba and Puerto Rico). They will be submitted to the Symposium of CEHME, the Center for the Study of History of Freemasonry in Spain and its former colonies (https://cehme.com/). One of them discusses the quarterly journal *ACACIA*, of Grand Lodge of Puerto Rico (https://web.cortland.edu/romeu/TrabajoCEHME-Ceuta2023.pdf) which has, in more than one way, several points in common with our own newspaper, *The Word*.

ACACIA started its quarterly publications in the summer of 1924. It had a booklet format, with 32 pages, no adds, and three fixed sections (Editorial, Message from the GM, and English section), plus articles submitted by the readers. Its English section was intended for the many American Masons residing in the Island (Grand Lodge of PR had two American Grand Masters: William Lippitt and C. Elmendorf). Articles were classified into three groups: dealing with news about the Grand Lodge and its members, dealing with Masonic education, esoterism and ritual, and dealing with Masonic activities that impacted the community and the society they served.

Grand Lodge of Puerto Rico has long fostered such community activities. For example, GMPerez Rios wrote in his *ACACIA* Message (Fall/1975): "Masonic temples may be used, instead of once a week, also every day, as libraries, community centers, medical dispensaries, recreation centers for the elderly, etc.. This way, the Lodge would be integrated with community needs." It is important to understand that, in Puerto Rico, social services are inferior to those we have here.

ACACIA stopped publication during the mid-2010s. After Hurricane Maria of 2017 and the default of the island's government, there was no longer enough money to sustain the publication.

And here is where we would like to bring up, again, the topic of our newspaper *The Word*.

In addition to what we wrote in our Mentor column of October 2022, regarding *The Word*, we can add the following: our newspaper is the main means of communication, and contact with Freemasonry, of our elderly members, as some seldom attend Lodge. Then, Winter Birds spend the cold months of the year out of state. Without *The Word*, these have no way of finding out what is going on in our District. With it, they feel that they can still participate in Craft affairs.

But the current growth of publication costs will soon make it difficult to support *The Word*. We need to find ways to save, or to increase, revenues. And there are several options available.

One is to email as many copies as possible, saving in postage and handling. But many of our older members do not have email accounts, or prefer to receive the written version. This option is thence, limited. Another option would raise current subscription and advertisement rates — but not so much that prices would scare away subscribers and advertisers. Finally, neighboring Districts could be invited to join us in receiving *The Word*. For example, the Oneida and Broome districts, which include Utica and Binghamton, could be interested, and would share in the expenses.

We don't have much time left to take action about this; otherwise we will follow *ACACIA*.

Jorge L. Romeu
Onondaga District Mentoring Chair

The Mentoring Corner

August 2023

Hello, Brethren:

The June issue of The Word carried the article "Memorials to Great Men who were Masons", reproduced from The Builder, February 1923. This article contains at least two worthy lessons. One lesson is about the importance of Masonic Journalism; the second lesson is about the influential standing of some members of The Craft, in yester years.

Said article was published a century ago and is still used today by Masonic papers like *The Word* and by Masonic and general historians, to assess events that occurred at the time. We hope that one hundred years from now, historians may also be interested in examining *The Word* to find out more about our life. Our newspaper is certainly a document full of information about our Lodge activities, as well as about present-day events that affect life in Central New York.

The second lesson reflects on the caliber of Membership at the time. Bro. Stephen Girard is profiled in much detail. He was a self-made millionaire and philanthropist, that donated large sums of money to many charities, colleges, and even lent money to the US government!

These days we are trying to increase our dwindling membership by using advanced web and marketing campaigns to recruit and retain members. Said methods address individuals who have inquired about Freemasonry -but we need to reach everybody! Let's examine this issue further.

Much has changed during the past 150 years in American society. At that time, there was no health or social security insurance. Some joined The Craft because of the economic protection it provided. Others joined to meet and befriend quality men with whom socialize or do business, outside their Lodges, or to pursue public endeavors of importance. All these legitimate reasons did not exclude their desire to become better men and enjoy the rich Masonic rituals.

Freemasonry was, and still is, a "big tent" organization. It has its core values of *Brotherly Love, Relief and Truth*, and pursues, as its main objective, "making some good men, better".

But we must also consider additional features to offer our members, such as fellowship, networking, comprehensive self-improvement programs, and possibilities for our members to develop their talents and activities of interest, sports, readings, hobbies, do community work, and engage in family events. In England some Lodges are organized into said activities. In New

York we have only two types of specialties: Research and Observant Masonry. Maybe we need more.

When I came to CNY 43 years ago, many towns had an independent newspaper where folks read all sorts of opinions about most topics. Today, the majority have closed or were absorbed by limited mainstream media organizations that avoid difficult topics or treat them unbalanced, thus contributing to tearing apart the fiber of our country and exacerbating hostile public discourse.

The Craft has an opportunity to show that it takes seriously our *Love of Country* tenant. It can provide our communities *nonpartisan forums*, where important topics can be developed with *tolerance and civility*. This participation would bring The Craft a well-earned reputation among our neighbors, that may entice some to join an Institution that enriches Civil Society.

Jorge L. Romeu
Onondaga District Mentoring Chair

The Mentoring Corner

September 2023

Hello, Brethren:

This month I would like to talk about *charity*, and about *doing the right thing*. Personally, I prefer the word *solidarity*, in lieu of charity. To me, it sounds much kinder.

There are, at least, two types of *Masonic charities*: institutional and local. And both have strong features and advantages. *Institutional* are those organized and directed by the upper ranks of our organizations (Grand Lodge or Appended Body). For example, the

Brotherhood Fund and the Masonic Medical Research Institute are operated by Grand Lodge. And the Dyslexia Centers are managed by the Scottish Rite, NMJ. They all provide a valuable service to our society.

Projects such as those mentioned could not be organized and supported by a local Lodge or a Valley, as they require a level of capital and manpower, way beyond their means. However, I ask myself sometimes, how many people out there are really aware that said projects are maintained by Freemasons? For, these projects operate far away from most people's own communities.

The other types of projects are *local* ones. These are operated by local Lodges or Valleys in their own communities, and we have excellent examples here in Central New York: pantries are filled with donations, sometimes distributed by Lodges; ramps for the disabled are built at their homes; Easter Egg hunts and Santa parties are organized at Lodge premises; Children ID project*, conducted at State Fair; college fairs for High School students; blood donation drives, etc., all are free in our communities. The advantage with local projects is that our friends an neighbors know us, and connect them with Freemasonry. They are also excellent promotion and recruitment tool!

The other issue I wanted to bring up is *doing the right thing.* The problem with this proposal is that *the right thing can be different, for different people*. For example, one person may support candidate A, while another may support candidate B, because they like their proposed programs.

Freemasonry has an excellent tool to deal with such apparent contradiction: Tolerance. One can strongly disagree with someone else's point of view, and still may have a civil exchange of ideas. We should try to understand where people are coming from, and what are their strong and weak points, for usually issues are not totally right, nor totally wrong. This should help us find a middle ground, where we can all function together. After all, we are all here for the duration!

For example, two persons sitting in opposite corners of a room, looking at a statue paced in the center, will see different features. One may see the front better; the other may see the back.

There is an old story about four blind men tapping an elephant in different parts of its body. The one touching the foot thinks it is a big tree; the one touching the trunk thinks it is a big hose.They were all right, because *their reality* is established according to *their perspective*. Maybe the solution is to help people see the totality, instead of just the individual parts of a problem or of an issue. Freemasonry, with its tolerance, may be of help in trying to reconcile different positions.

Freemasonry is more than just some good men improving themselves, and forming lasting relationships. Some of such *improved men* may also want to help improve their surroundings. Freemasonry provides such Brethren with an outlet, to help them pursue this work.

Jorge L. Romeu
Onondaga District Mentoring Chair

* The Masonic Child ID (Identification) Program, which was also for adults, is no longer supported by Grand Lodge, and is generally done today by kits and phone apps.

The Mentoring Corner
October 2023

Hello, Brethren:

This month I visited the website of the Scottish Rite Research Society, where I found an interesting essay on *The Future of Freemasonry*, by Bro. Angel Millar. This is a very important topic for our Institution. We had 350,000 members in the 1920s. And today, one hundred years later, we do not reach 30,000! Bro. Millar's essay is in: http://scottishriteresearch.com/wp-content/uploads/2020/04/
SRRS-The-Plumbline-Winter-2019-Angel-Millar.pdf

According to Bro. Millar, nearly 90% of Freemasons believe that Masonic education is important, or very important, and that nearly one-in-four Brethren who feel unsatisfied, are not finding much inclination toward spirituality, philosophy, education, research, or history. He says that Masonic education should not try to compete with academia. Instead, our talks should be relevant to those listening, providing new insights into their internal struggles and lives. Millar adds that not every brother may be interested in esoteric. Instead, talks about wartime and other experiences, that illustrates core Masonic values of brotherhood, may also be very effective.

In New York City, for example, there is an initiative called "Brothers for Brothers." Said program, according to its founder, Bro. Teodorescu, will offer an internal platform for Masons to foster, develop and enhance qualities of well-rounded upright men, via suitable mentorship and knowledge sharing. Presentations may be on practical life skills: communication skills, or other personal and professional development, confidence and self-esteem, health issues, etc.. Presenters may be brothers who have such an expertise, or have earned a university degree in these subjects.

Another type of event, adds Bro. Millar, that brought people to Ezekiel Lodge, in Mass, are called *MasonicCon*. They feature various speakers and host vendors of Masonic merchandise. In Pasadena CA, a MasonicCon had three days of speakers, panels, screenings, vendors, and a pop culture festive board. Attendance to such annual events may help keep Masons in the fraternity.

Today, continues Bro. Millar, there are new challenges, new Brothers, new social needs to be satisfied, and a new attitude. Freemasonry is changing: "People today are busy, and time is precious. The lodge has to be a place of experience more meaningful than that of everyday life".

Bro. Millar ends by stating that Freemasonry should focus on *three key areas: understanding symbolism and history, fostering a non-sectarian, non-dogmatic environment*, where all Masons can participate, and *fostering camaraderie* and strong bonds of brotherhood.

This Mentor has stated, from these columns, how there are at least three non-excluding key areas in The Craft: *ritual, fellowship and service*. Masons enjoy and participate in all three, but tend to emphasize one of them. Some Brethren emphasize on *rituals*, where we learn the positive values that Freemasonry teaches us for our improvement, or that emphasize both our *esoteric* and *historical* components. They have special (research, observant) Lodges, or develop them in their own Lodges. *Fellowship* has always been a key component of Freemasonry: here we make and keep many of our best and life-long friends. Finally, *service to humanity*, one of our core values, is often developed through community projects, for the benefit of our friends and neighbors.

We received an invitation from GL Leadership and Educational Services Committee, for the *All in Call: a Grand Lodge of New York Weekend of Service Planning*, hosted on line, Sunday October 8, at 7:00 PM. MWGM Kessler says that, over the last two years, our Fraternity has provided services that made a difference in the lives of others. GM is instituting the Weekend of Service November 11th and 12th. The on-line Statewide planning call will prepare such event.

Jorge L. Romeu
Onondaga District Mentoring Chair

The Mentoring Corner

November 2023

Hello, Brethren:

December is the month when we bid farewell to the current year and prepare to receive the New Year: it is a renewal time! Most cultures and most religions have special events to commemorate such departure and arrival, always looking forward to the future with optimism. We wish all our Brethren and their families a Happy New Year, with health and peace!

This month, we want to talk about the *Word Readership Survey* we sent out last month. Have you filled yours out and sent it back, yet? We have received only 30, from our 2200 readers, but we need many more so its results are valid. We will explain the survey a bit more in this column.

The first question "How do you receive it" helps us validate it. We know that approximately 90% receive the word by mail. A valid survey will provide Mail responses close to this number.

We then embark into specifics about the readership habits: how often do readers peruse the different sections of the newspaper. *Always and Frequently* are excellent. *Seldom* is still OK, if such section is not specifically related to your District, or Appended Body. *Never* is an indicator of little interest in said section. When Never is high one can investigate why this is occurring and how, if in any way, it can be improved. Even if a reader does not belong to an Appended Body, there may be an article about what it does, how it works, etc., that can attract general interest.

In every issue, the word publishes several sections of general interest. *Special Readings* are reprinted from *The Builder* or other reputable Masonic sources. Other sections are the *Editor's Prerogative*, Mentor and EMESBE. We want to assess how they arise our readers' interest.

The Calendar of Events resulted one of the preferred sections, based on the 30 surveys so far received, and it makes sense. For, once we find out what is going on in our District, we want to select, plan and schedule which ones, of said chosen events and activities, we can actually attend.

We ask for readers' Masonic affiliation. In addition to Blue Lodge for men, and to Eastern Star for women, we may also belong to one or more appended bodies. Some Brothers are also into the Eastern Star. We can assess the extent of involvement by the number of bodies that a member belongs to. Some are only in Blue Lodge. Others also belong to one or more Appended Bodies. This doesn't necessarily mean that these have a deeper involvement -just that they are more widely extended. One can be a Blue Lodge Mason and have a significant participation in one's Lodge and District. Alternatively, one can be a sideliner in several Appended Bodies.

We can use this additional information to assess whether some body members prefer or avoid specific types of reading (say, for example, that Scottish Rite members prefer historical articles from *The Builder*, while York Rite members prefer to read the *Editor's Prerogative*).

We asked for years as members of The Craft (not your age). We can also correlate the type of readings with membership (say, for example, that newer members prefer to read *EMESBE*).

We received interesting comments in some survey forms. A frequent one regarded the letters from their Lodges. Several Brothers complained about not always being able to read news about their Lodges (because said articles were not sent to the Editor). For, residing out of town, said Lodge letters, plus other general information in *The Word*, made them feel much closer to home.

Some readers said they preferred to receive and read the hard copy newspaper, and that they were willing to pay some more for it, since they do understand that mailing the paper costs more. Placing a yearly Ad in the word may help: a full year, small, sponsor Ad costs only $33.

The initial survey results are https://web.cortland.edu/romeu/PublishedSurveyData.pdf

Jorge L. Romeu
Onondaga District Mentoring Chair

The Mentoring Corner
December 2023

Hello, Brethren:

This month I planned to write about the excellent article, *World-Wide Masonry and its Desirability*, by Bro. Oliver Day Street, that our Editor reprinted from *The Builder* (June 1923) and published in November issue of *The Word*. Bro. Street, a seasoned Masonic researcher, wrote the book "Symbolism of the Three Degrees", accessible in the National Masonic Library web page: http://www.phoenixmasonry.org/symbolism_of_the_three_degrees.htm

But MWGM Aníbal Rosario Ruiz, of the Grand Lodge of Puerto Rico, informed us Brethren in his November weekly message, that the Vatican's Doctrinal office had declared, on November 15th, that: "Active membership in Freemasonry by a member of the faithful is prohibited, because of the irreconcilability between Catholic doctrine and Freemasonry". Pope Francis, who is Jesuit, approved said declaration, that can be read in https://www.reuters.com/world/europe/vatican-confirms-ban-catholics-becoming-freemasons-2023-11-15/.

Such Catholic Church position is not new. In 1983, Cardinal Ratzinger, at the time Prefect of the Congregation for the Doctrine of the Faith, who later became Pope Benedict XVI, stated in a declaration on Freemasonry that "the faithful who enroll in Masonic associations are in a state of grave sin, and may not receive Holy Communion." This information is also available in the web: https://www.vatican.va/roman_curia/congregations/cfaith/documents/rc_con_cfaith_doc_19831126_declaration-masonic_en.html and was approved by John Paul II, who was Pope at the time.

However, within the Catholic Church itself, there is no unanimity regarding its relationships with Freemasonry. The article *New Openings to Make Masonic Membership Permissible* has a good discussion on this subject's history, and shows several examples of prominent lay Catholics as well as of priests, who are also Freemasons. Said article is also available in the internet: https://insidethevatican.com/magazine/new-openings-to-make-masonic-membership-permissible/?gclid=Cj0KCQiAsburBhCIA-RIsAExmsu7InIPEMHBhF31yiW5Y7M1IsNG2uznsLTHgKib4vV SzCjOMCbJuQ8YaAjTGEALw_wcB)

This Mentor is both a practicing Catholic and Mason and has sung in his Parish Choir, every week, for over thirty years. We have never perceived any contradiction between these two issues. Moreover, we find that belonging to one strengthens our participation in the other. In our native Cuba, as well as in Puerto Rico and in the Dominican Republic, where Catholics constitute the majority among religious faiths, the number of Catholics who are also Freemasons, is profuse.

Perhaps said attitude of exclusion stems from another reason. In Latin America, the Spanish colonial regime and the King itself, were strongly supported by the dominant Catholic Church. In said countries, conservatives and colonial regime sympathizers found support within the Catholic Church, and liberals and pro-independence sympathizers found support in their Masonic Lodges.

There is a Spanish research organization called CEHME (Center for the Study of the History of Freemasonry in Spain and its Colonies), founded by Dr. Ferrer Benimeli, a Jesuit priest whose doctoral dissertation on Freemasonry started this research movement. CEHME includes scores of researchers, both Academic and Freemasons, who present their findings in periodic conferences, which are later published in its proceedings. In its most recent conference this Mentor presented a paper on *ACACIA*, the official quarterly journal of the Grand Lodge of Puerto Rico, that will be one Century old next year.

Cooperation, instead of confrontation, is possible, and more positive!

Jorge L. Romeu
Onondaga District Mentoring Chair

2024

The Mentoring Corner

January 2024

Hello, Brethren:

I reviewed the article *World-Wide Masonry and its Desirability*, by Bro. Oliver Day Street, reprinted from *The Builder* (June 1923) and published in our November issue of *The Word*. Bro. Street was a Masonic researcher and writer, and a Foreign Correspondent. His book "Symbolism of the Three Degrees", is accessible in the National Masonic Library. This article is seminal, especially for those interested in the procedural and practical development of our Craft.

The main topic is the creation of a Universal Masonry. Bro. Street states: "There is not, never has been, and never will be". Then he discusses some of the main reasons why it doesn't happen, which may be summarized into religious, membership, politics and hierarchical. He says:

"Some Grand Lodges admittedly recognize only those grand bodies which speak English; others while not professing this standard, made it good in practice. Some draw a line on those which do not quite agree with them on some religious dogma, or as to just how far Masonry may take part in the political questions of the day, or on some rule of mere practice or policy on which uniformity has never existed among the recognized Masonic bodies".

Let's analyze how these issues fair:

Some masonic bodies, such as the Grand Orient de France, do not require a belief in God. It is enough to believe in abstract goodness. Other bodies allow *Mixed Lodges*: men and women can belong jointly to them. Other bodies have a very political attitude and, in some cases, have developed revolutionary activities. And other bodies, especially in Europe and some countries in South America, have *a pyramidal structure* whereby the Supreme Council controls, not only its four bodies, but also the "Blue" Lodges. In the United States, England, Cuba, Puerto Rico, DR, and others, these are *kept separate* and *govern themselves independently*. Finally, the doctrine of exclusive territorial jurisdiction, whereby a single Grand Lodge can exist in a nation or territory.

Bro. Street does not judge these positions but proposes to engage in a dialogue to understand them better: "We must be willing to meet and discuss these questions with them, and maybe we shall find we are not so far apart after all." He suggests the organization of "a World Masonic Conference, a consultative movement which would bring together with them Masons or bodies which they have not already formally recognized as legitimate and regular Freemasonry."

There have been *some efforts* in such direction: the Conference of Grand Masters of North America https://www.cogmna.info/ and Inter-American Masonic Confederation, both of which we have discussed in this column before. Find International Masonic Organizations around the world in: https://freemasonry.network/masonic-structures/international-masonic-organizations/

Bro. Street traveled the world as a Foreign Correspondent, and visited Lodges all over. He encourages Masons to visit them, to learn how they operate. and suggests taking five measures:

> "First, that the International Masonic Association, at Geneva, Switzerland, be supported and developed; Secondly, we already have one, in the National Masonic Research Society, of Iowa; Thirdly, our Committees on Foreign Correspondence should endeavor to get facts and lay them before their respective Grand Lodges; Fourthly, intelligent Masons visiting foreign countries should be encouraged to visit the lodges there and get first-hand information, Fifthly, a World Congress of Freemasons should be held periodically, say every five years, to collect and share information about Freemasonry in different nations and regions, without judging or otherwise."

This is a profound article, worth not only of reading, but also of discussing in open Lodge.

Jorge L. Romeu
Onondaga District Mentoring Chair

The Mentoring Corner
February 2024

Hello, Brethren:

I just can't keep up with our Editor, no matter how much I try! He includes, in every issue of *The Word*, more excellent articles, taken from *The Builder*, than I can review!

In the December issue, he published *Patriotism — as interpreted by Freemasonry*, written by the WM of Lodge No. 524, in Evanston, IL. Its Master asked to remain anonymous and, instead, give credit to his Lodge Education Committee. Said Lodge delivered, once a month, an address on challenging topics such as: Initiation, Fraternity, Toleration, Faith, Truth, Charity, Morality, Patriotism, Symbolism, Philosophy, Happiness and Immortality. The article, which shows a good example worth replicating, was taken from the December 1923 issue of The Builder magazine.

We often forget that, in our Investiture when we become Lodge Masters, we pledge to have, in every meeting, one learning activity, However, more often than not, this is not realized.

Said article on Patriotism starts by defining what this word means. The dictionary tells us that a patriot is "one whose ruling passion is the love of his country" and that patriotism is "love and zeal for one's country". The article then explains that "patriotism must be founded on great principles, supported by great virtues, that it involves duties as well as privileges, and that these duties rise in connection with the domestic relations of the citizen to his country as well as in all that concerns the attitude of the country towards foreign nations." The article ends by stating: "The highest lesson taught to us as a Craft, by the Freemasons of the American Revolution, is to place patriotism above partisanship, to preserve and extend the free institutions of the Republic".

Patriotism is not only offering our lives to defend our country. Patient citizenship work, such as fostering civil exchanges between competing political groups, providing sound information to voters, and enhancing tolerance for dissimilar ideas, helps strengthen our institutions and values.

As Freemasons, we profess our *love of country*, and commit to *undertaking service* to all humanity. Freemasonry, one of the oldest members of Civil Society, needs to transfer such love of country and commitment to service into practical action, and help society to become better.

Individually, Masons will do this, usually with limited results. As an Institution, efforts are multiplied manyfold. Without taking sides in political debate, which is against our charter, our Institution can greatly contribute in two ways. First, Masons could sponsor open debates in their premises, as long as participants are willing to behave with civility and be tolerant of different ideas. Secondly, Masons could organize talks providing factual information about key issues. It is unfortunate that some media sources are partisan, and provide incorrect or biased information. If people are better informed about issues and their consequences, the atmosphere will improve.

Many years from now, when most of us are no longer around, our grandchildren may ask: what was Freemasonry doing during the *uncivil times*? It would be very sad to answer: Nothing!

This is a very sensitive topic, that needs to be discussed and thought through, very seriously. This Mentor proposes that a group of interested Brethren is formed, and then starts talking about whether this is worth doing, and, if so, how could it be best implemented, by whom, when, etc..

One way to do this is through Zoom meetings. We can initially meet on the First Tuesday of every month, starting on March 5th, at 7 pm, for getting organized. We can use the Zoom link: https://syracuseuniversity.zoom.us/j/94545765754 and the phone (646)876-9923 (in New York). We can use the same link, every First Tuesday of the month. There is no Password: just click in!

Jorge L. Romeu
Onondaga District Mentoring Chair

Letter to the CNY DDGMs Regarding the Previous Article

Syracuse, 15 February 2024

A Proposal for Central New York Districts to contribute to defuse uncivil discourse.

Dear DDGMs, Lodge Masters and Brothers all:

We have all seen an unfortunate deterioration in the national political conversation, that produces very unfavorable results. Internally, it debases our political institutions and the public faith in them; abroad, it raises concerns about the American reliability, among US allies and partners, and induces America's enemies to believe that the time may be appropriate to act against us, as we are too divided.

We are Masons; and as such, we assert our commitment to "love of country" and "service to humanity" (and humanity begins at home). I believe the time has come to put said assertions to practice.

I am attaching my Mentor article for the forthcoming issue of *The Word*, that discusses this issue in more detail. And I am proposing that those of us interested in this endeavor start talking about whether it is suitable to do something, and if so, what, when, where, by whom, how, etc..

I am proposing that me meet in the Internet this coming Tuesday, March 5th, at 7 pm, for discussing further this idea, using the Zoom link: https://syracuseuniversity.zoom.us/j/94545765754 And if we agree it is worthwhile, that we keep meeting, using the same Zoom link, every First Tuesday of the month until election day.

I am asking the DDGMs of our Central New York Districts to consider my proposal. And if you believe it is appropriate, that you forward this email, with the attached Word article, to your Lodge Masters, asking these Lodge Masters to make the material available to their Lodge Brethren.

I thank you in advance for your time, consideration, and help with this project.

Respectfully and Fraternally,

Jorge Luis Romeu, MM
Past Master, Liverpool Syracuse Lodge No. 501
Membership Chair, Onondaga Masonic District.

The Mentoring Corner

March 2024

Hello, Brethren:

In the past, this MENTOR has written columns about Freemasonry in Cuba and P.R., during the XIX Century (e.g. May 2021). We will now quickly overview the XX Century.

During the first 40 years after Cuba became independent (in 1902), Freemasonry developed firmly throughout the island. Most every town had its own one-story Lodge building and the big cities had more than one. Havana, whose metropolitan area had 25% of the country's population, included about 1/3 of all Cuban Lodges, plus the Appended Bodies and the Grand Lodge. Many social, political and economic public figures: government ministers, university deans, newspaper editors, business executives etc., joined and several became Grand Masters. It was its golden age.

Leading town figures, such as doctors, judges, pharmacists, schoolteachers, chief of police, mayor, political boss, even the priest, usually became members. Many local and national issues were informally considered. My father joined one of these Lodges in a provincial city, in 1926.

After 1940 the economic situation of the country improved, and Freemasonry spread much faster, doubling in members and Lodges. The new Lodge buildings had now two-stories: the first floor was rented out for income, and the Lodge used the second one. A Grand Lodge skyscraper was built in Havana, using three floors for Lodges and the Masonic university, and renting the rest. More social, political and economic public figures joined, enhancing its public standing.

But the government's political corruption and mismanagement was creating an unhealthy environment. Freemasonry and other civil society groups failed to help improve this situation. It led to a broad loss of faith in the Cuban governmental system. Such loss in turn brought the 1959 revolution, as many thought a new generation would help fix our national problems (at the time, Marxism was not part of said fix). However, the remedy resulted even worse than the disease!

The revolutionary government took over all private enterprise, education system, and media, and banned all political parties. Citizens were required to fill long forms known as "cuentame tu vida" (tell me the story of your life) where religious and fraternal activities, past work history, all family abroad or jailed, etc., was requested. Individual future work and study opportunities were offered, depending on such information. Those classified as "non supporters" were ignored.

Freemasonry was never banned, as occurred in Russia, Germany or Spain, for our Craft had a long and distinguished history forging the Cuban nation; but it was severely affected. Masonic Lodges were required to submit to the Ministry of Interior, within 72 hours after each session, a report detailing who was present, what matters were discussed, etc.. Hence, between the tens of thousands who left the country and those who ended or decreased their Lodge attendance due to political measures penalizing participation, the participation of younger and economically active members substantially decreased. These measures were effective enough to choke Lodges. It was during this time that I joined The Craft, after two years of military service in the labor units.

Such situation lasted until mid-1980s, when Cuban government allowed religious believers and Masons to join official institutions, and pressure on membership and attendance eased up. It is possible that our past Cuban experience predisposes this Mentor to advocate on behalf of a more activist stance of our Craft that contributes toward a healthier political environment.

Thus, Mentor will offer a Zoom talk on Surveys and their implementation and interpretation, on Tuesday April 2nd, at 7 pm, using link https://syracuseuniversity.zoom.us/j/94545765754

Jorge L. Romeu;
Onondaga District Mentoring Chair

The Mentoring Corner
April 2024

Hello, Brethren:

Last week, in our monthly Scottish Rite exec committee meeting, over a dozen Brothers from all Districts served by *The Word* discussed relevant issues. There, it came up that our membership is thinning and graying. Such is not good for our long-term institutional health.

The Word Lodge letters document that these are developing activities that keep its members happy, thus achieving *retention*. But we need other activities to entice our profane neighbors to visit our Lodges: this is *recruiting*. One way to achieve this is by developing activities of general interest, making them available to the community. This will give us greater visibility.

With such intention in mind, Mentor offered a Zoom presentation about Surveys, on Tuesday, April 2nd. We had more attendees than in our first Zoom. But we need from our Brothers not only to attend said Zoom, but also to share its information with neighbors, so it becomes a community, rather than a purely Masonic event. Here is a proposed plan of action to help accomplish our goal.

A District committee of Lodge Masters could choose topics of general interest, neglected by media, such as providing not partisan explanations of how gerrymandering and electoral colleges work. District Lodge Members would attend and invite friends and members of other community organizations (VFW, Legion, Rotarians, etc.), thus attaining a critical mass for said event. Zooms may constitute an initial phase; but our key goal is to develop Lodge events to attract visitors.

The prevalent toxic levels in our society are reflected in a recent NPR/Marist poll, that found that 20%+ of Americans believe that resorting to violence will get the country back into its track. Freemasonry has a unique opportunity to help. Civil Society (community of its citizens linked by similar interests and collective activity) of which our Institution is a principal member, to act as a connecting link between the state and the public. Other Civil Society affiliates develop special (and legitimate) interests, such as promoting business, enhancing networks, etc.. *Freemasonry*, in turn, is *an ethical Institution*, whose professed goal is *to make some good men better*. This tenet calls on the Craft to lead in the promotion of values such as open-mindedness and tolerance.

We can get free access to TV channels, neighborhood newspapers, Library, and other media where public events are advertised. Initially, our attendance may be low. But if events are held consistently, attendance will increase. Topics could be diverse: history, travel, health, books, etc.. Invitation should be offered to speakers willing to abide by rational debate rules and respect. One significant objective of such an exercise is to encourage positive examples of public behavior.

There may be other approaches that would also accomplish these goals. They could be tried by different Districts, sharing experiences, and comparing results. In engineering, *pilot programs* are first developed; then, their results are compared, before implementing the final strategy.

This Mentor plans to give another Zoom on Tuesday, May 14th at 7 PM to consider possible topics for future talks and presentations: link https://syracuseuniversity.zoom.us/j/95700563555 We are actively seeking the input and advice from interested Brethren, especially Lodge leaders.

Finally, on a personal note, some already know that my son suffered a severe accident while vacationing in Puerto Rico. He spent one week in an ICU there, and another one in Miami. One issue about being a Mason is that we can always resort to our Brothers, when we are in distress. I contacted the Grand Lodge of PR, of which I am a dual member, and several Brothers in Miami, for information and assistance. It provided us with great comfort to see that we were not alone.

Jorge L. Romeu;
Onondaga District Mentoring Chair

Strengthening the Masonic Fraternity

Craftsmen OnLine, July 2024

{On June 2024 we were drafted into the GLNY Committee on Membership Growth. We wrote the following Essay, which can be

found at https://craftsmenonline.com/strengthening-the-masonic-fraternity/ }

The purpose of our Masonic Fraternity has always been "to make some good men better". Freemasonry encourages its members to improve themselves, and to establish strong links among each other. In addition, some of these better men have felt a call to improve their communities, making Freemasonry a valuable asset for society. However, this important aspect doesn't seem to be well understood by some. In this article we examine this situation further.

Let's consider three fundamental factors: (1) the state of our contemporary society, (2) the nature of our Institution, and (3) the different types of Freemasons.

First, contemporary society has ceased to be as gregarious as it used to be. Computers, cell phones, and other such media devices foster individuality. As a result, most organizations, professional societies, churches, unions and clubs, have seen their membership decline.

The second factor is the nature of our Institution. Organizations acquire an unwritten contract with its members, to make good use of their time and resources. After we raise a Brother, do we provide further masonic education, substantial fellowship events, or further involvement in community work? Attending Lodge to discuss budget issues does not raise much interest. Providing lectures or training on useful topics (e.g., internet, computers, software) will help Brethren succeed in the profane world.

The third factor is the type of member, as not everyone is the same, likes the same things, or has joined our Craft for the same reasons. For example, some join in search of fellowship; and find it in our meetings and social activities. Others join to acquire esoteric experiences, and they find it in our Observant and Research Lodges. Still others, join to improve themselves — and some of these, may also want to help improve society at large.

One way to increase our visibility is by developing community projects. Grand Lodge has several national projects such as the Masonic Medical Research Lab. But Freemasonry, like politics, is Local. Our community needs to know what we are doing for them: developing a food pantry; providing Thanksgiving and Christmas meals; Breakfast with Santa; Easter egg-hunts; a career day for high school kids; building ramps for the disabled ...

These few examples of projects give the Craft more visibility in our communities. They do not cost much, but require work, which can also help increase Lodge fellowship and participation.

We can also open our Lodges for selected activities, inviting friends and neighbors to participate and see what we do. It is sometimes difficult to explain that we are not a secret, but a discrete organization. A better way is by having people visit our Lodges.

Lodges can organize public activities, such as documentaries about travel, especially during our long winters. Lodges can develop presentations about identifying drug problems, or potential health issues, and about ways to resolve community problems. We have Brothers with many backgrounds, that allow them to address these issues.

Most Lodges have a multipurpose room, where social events can be prepared, using a projector, computer, sound system, etc.. A District-wide lists of lecturers can be established to find speakers. Offer coffee and donuts. Some topics may have been already presented elsewhere. But our neighbors may prefer to hear a speaker they know, and can relate to.

After the presentations, invite the audience to visit the Lodge room, and have a Brother answer questions. Advertise events in the local newspaper and radio stations. Join forces with other local organizations: Rotary, Lyons, VFW, the library, etc., and with other local Lodges.

Finally, work with DeMolay, Rainbow Girls and other youth groups. Provide them with interesting activities such as camping, canoeing, bowling, as well as training in practical things (computers, exam reviews, etc.). They will grow up and eventually join ...

Such things help members develop an increased and stronger Lodge involvement. People usually respond positively to groups activities. Project work creates stronger fellowship bonds.

The Craft will attain higher visibility in our own communities. Friends and neighbors will have a different outlook of who we are, and what we do. Community work may become the best promotion of our Craft, and an efficient recruiting tool. For, some of these neighbors and friends, participating in our activities, may want to know more about us, and eventually join the Craft.

Planning, preparing and carrying out of such activities and projects will take extra time and energy, from our Lodge members. But such activities will also contribute to retain them.

Some other Masonic writers have proposed radical changes to our Craft, that reminds me of the saying "you are throwing away the baby with the bath water". Maybe, losing members will help us think through all these issues, and come up with efficient answers.

The Mentoring Corner
August 2024

Hello, Brethren:

If you have followed this column for the past two years, you will have noticed two recurring themes: the toxic state of our politics, and the situation with our paper, *The Word*.

During these two summer months, we have seen much movement concerning toxic political environment. Accusations, name-calling, insults and the use of four-letter words continue. All this created the environment that generated an attempt assassination of a presidential candidate!

I am old enough to remember when politicians of different persuasions were not enemies but contenders, and that their political programs were not national threats, but proposed solutions to the national problems. Politicians posted, in addition to their head-shots and names, their party affiliation and their positions regarding key issues, in their political posters. The media had two separate sections: news and opinion, and outstanding journalists, such as Cronkite, McNeil, and Lehrer, educated their audiences about the important topics, instead of increasing their divisions.

As Freemasons, irrespective of whether we are Democrats, Republicans or independents, we espouse tolerance and brotherly love. We need to actively promote love of country and a reasoned partisan politics in our communities, if we want to preserve our democratic system.

Then, comes our newspaper: *The Word*. During the two summer months, we created a group (Bros. Ben Lees, Shawn Trauff, Brian Courtney, Steve Zabriskie and this Mentor) to revise and update our newspaper management system and its tools. We expect, by bringing this system to the XXI Century, to resolve all the subscribers' updating and billing issues, to their satisfaction.

Having a Masonic newspaper is a great idea, in addition to a distinctive honor. Readers can find out what is going on in their Lodge and District, as well as in others of their interest. News about forthcoming events, where we may want to participate, are posted. Readings of edifying topics, reproduced from *The Builder* by our Editor, are always included. *The Word* is especially useful to our older members, who may not always be able to attend Lodge, and to our snowbirds and our confined elderly who, by reading the news, can feel engaged in our Masonic endeavors.

There are high-ranking brothers in our Grand Lodge who periodically read our paper, find it of interest and quality, and would perhaps like to see more of them appear, using ours as model.

Finally, this Mentor is now also a member of the Retention Training Team Committee that will advise GLNY on ways to augment and retain our membership. I believe that increasing our Lodge-Community participation will foster recruitment and enhance retainment. In engineering, when implementing new approaches, one first tries them in a small prototype, to assess if/how they work. Here, such prototype would consist of a group of Lodges, where we can implement these ideas, assess whether they have enhanced recruitment and retention, and compare its results with those of other Lodges/Districts, where such new methods have not yet been implemented.

Some approaches to try out would include developing local community projects; organizing public events and inviting our friends and neighbors to participate; working with DeMolay and other masonic youth groups. Many Brothers have backgrounds that allow them to address these issues. Advertise these events in the local media, and join forces with other local organizations, such as the American Legion, VFW, Rotary, Lions, the Public Library, and so forth.

A group of interested brothers have had a Zoom meeting to talk about it. We plan to have more. If you are interested in joining, please contact this Mentor [email redacted].

Jorge L. Romeu
Onondaga District Mentoring Chair

The Mentoring Corner

September 2024

Hello, Brethren:

During the month of August, we participated in initial meetings of the *Retention Training Team Committee* that advises GLNY on membership recruitment and retainment and in *group of brothers interested in developing community projects in our Lodges* (we have the second exchange on September 10th). From these talks, several excellent ideas arose and were discussed.

One idea reviewed the efficient placement into Lodges, of candidates sent to us by NorthStar, which first requires two things. First, we need to collect more data from candidates, and from our Grand Lodge members. We need information about their occupations, levels of education, etc. to ascertain their potential interests. Second, lodges need to identify a 'specialty'. We have Research and Observant Masonry lodges, that specialize in ritual, historic and esoteric themes. But we also want to develop additional areas, such as sports (fishing, hunting, bicycling, etc.), arts (creating a choir, a band, giving conferences), etc.. Its members could then be identified at the District level.

Another great idea is assigning to each Candidate a social Mentor. They could sit together in sessions, clarifying what is happening in the Ritual, introducing said member to older ones, and providing general support. I still remember fondly my lodge Brother Frank Rosa, who performed such function for me when I joined Liverpool. Rosa later became one of my personal friends.

At the beginning, a candidate can be assigned to a *Lodge NorthStar mentor*, to instruct him in the topics he needs to learn, regarding the Three Degrees he is taking, and Freemasonry in general. During this process, other lodge members will interact with said candidate and, logically, some will develop more affinity than others. Persuade one of these, to become his *Lodge social mentor*.

These first two steps, which are not simple nor evident, will greatly contribute to retain those candidates that come to us through NorthStar, or that apply directly to our lodges. But we also need to do some activities in our community that allows us to become better known, and to bring in more local visitors to our Lodges. This is where the *Lodge community projects* come into play.

In yester years (e.g., during our grandfathers' days) life was very different than it is today. Communities were more stable, and neighbors knew each other from *way back*. Lodge members were recruited from our longtime friends and co-workers, our relatives, and our other community contacts. That lifestyle no longer exists. Candidates joining our lodges know few if anyone there.

Then, the most valuable item anyone possesses is *time*. We can lose or waste one dollar, and we can earn, inherit, or win another one in the lottery. The hour that we lose or waste will never be recovered. We need to offer the prospective member of our Fraternity a compelling reason to spend his valuable time with us. In our opinion, this is the *most important reason for attrition*.

Developing community activities and projects, that make our Craft known and bring visitors to our lodges will encourage others to join us. Then, developing new lodge activities and a strong sense of lodge community within our membership, will encourage them to remain with us.

Finally, we need to experiment with different versions of the ideas exposed above, in diverse lodges, then assess and compare their results, and verify what works and how, and what doesn't. This is what we engineers call *prototyping*, used to identify, select and improve our final plan.

A way to implement these ideas is what we are discussing in the Zoom meetings of the group of brothers interested in developing community projects in our lodges. We plan to have more of them. If you are interested in joining us, please contact this Mentor [email redacted].

Jorge L. Romeu
Onondaga District Mentoring Chair

The Mentoring Corner
October 2024

Hello, Brethren:

For several months, Mentor has written about the benefits of *developing community projects in our Lodges*, an idea that a group of interested brothers has discussed in several Zoom meetings.

This article develops a mini-blueprint that shows what such an effort would entail.

We can divide such project into three phases: *conceptualization, preparation and execution*. In the *conceptualization phase*, we start by *summoning all the district Lodges*, under their DDGM. The Masters, Wardens and Deacons (MWD) is the ideal local organization to Decide whether to start such a project, select a leader, and then determine the *Who, What, When, Where, and How*.

What project will we do? It should be something valuable for the community, that we can do and that has not been done before. Schools do "student fairs", presenting college careers. But not all students want or can attend college. Few student fairs discuss trades. Thence, they don't have much information about this topic. We also need to find qualified speakers, willing and able to talk about preparing for the different trades, and obtaining supporting information about them.

In the *preparation phase*, we need to *find a suitable Lodge*: one, centrally placed, with easy access, parking, and a pleasant venue to conduct the event. We need to *find external partners*, e.g., VFW, Rotary, etc., to join us. Make clear to them that *we are all partners* and have something to gain. Sometimes, organizations worry about working with others, for fear of losing membership. Create a *steering committee*, where all the groups are represented, contribute, and share the work.

Invite OES to collaborate; bring your wives and daughters. We are an organization of men. When developing an event that include women and children, mixed crowds make all feel at ease. Provide coffee and donuts, and don't proselytize with the guests. If they like us, some will ask to join. However, and much more important, guests will get to know us, which is our objective.

Arrange for publicity: newspapers, radio and TV stations promote local events for free. Each participating organization should contribute four or five attendees. Entering an empty room is not conducive to success. The first time around, there probably won't be many guests. Do Persevere! Spread the event news: secure a review in some local paper, or write your own for The Word and leave copies of our newspaper with the local libraries and with other community organizations.

In the *execution phase*, organize your room: have sufficient chairs and tables for guests, one for the brochures of all participating organizations, and for coffee, tea, etc.. Have some men and women at the door, to welcome guests. Have an MC introduce the event, have information and brochures available. Start the event on time and don't make it too lengthy. Announce follow-up events. Arrange a box, pads and pencils for attendees' comments; read their concerns to improve future events. Thank the public for attending, before they go home, and invite them again!

Another effective event topic is a student writing competition. Create a brochure with theme, prizes, etc.. Contact all area high schools and announce the event date. Conduct it at the Lodge room. Have a room and an activity for the accompanying parents, to wait until their kids finish writing their pieces. Recruit a serious reading committee to assess the compositions. Give cash prizes, and a diploma at the Lodge: make it a festive event, possibly with food and refreshments. Such event provides two opportunities to have kids' parents, relatives, and neighbors, visiting the Lodge. Our guests will see who we are, and what we do. Deeds are always better than words!

To join our Zoom meetings, discussing said projects contact me: [email redacted]

Jorge L. Romeu
Onondaga District Mentoring Chair

The Mentoring Corner
November 2024

Hello, Brethren:

Sometimes, wonderful things occur unexpectedly. This is what happened a couple of weeks ago, when I received email from RW LaRocco, director of the Grand Lodge Livingston Library requesting volunteers to open "Library Presentation Franchises" in Albany, Buffalo and Rochester. I applied, suggesting the Library opens a franchise in Syracuse. Bro. LaRocco agreed and now, our *Group Considering Lodge-Community activities* has found its first, important task.

Library Franchises would allow groups of Lodges, in said Upstate cities, to organize public talks about Freemasonry, similar to the ones offered each month by the Library in Grand Lodge. Said talks are filmed, and become excellent material to use in Lodge learning and discussion. Its videos can be found in: https://www.youtube.com/@thechancellorrobertrliving4946/featured

RW LaRocco's vision for such Francises consists in the creation of Masonic Centers around the State, that allow both Brothers and the public to attend live lectures, without having to travel to Grand Lodge. RW LaRocco's aim is to create a community of education, inquisitiveness and enlightenment, open to the public, that may help bring new members (recruitment), as well as to promote discussions among current Masons, that may help improve retention. These have been the same goals that our *Group that Explores Lodge-Community events* has been pursuing for the last several months. It is natural that we use said opportunity to establish our first public event.

During our Group Zoom, RW Bro. David Barnello described how their Lodge sponsored a program with the high school, where they would give some scholarship money to a student. The Lodge requested to be involved in the student selection process, which was denied by the school. Lodge then requested to be involved in the student award presentation, which was also denied. It was evident that the school wanted the scholarship money, but not anything else from the Lodge.

Several of us have had similar experiences, when dealing with non-masons. This may be a consequence of an atmosphere of distrust of Freemasonry, among some, that inhibits them from interacting with us. For some outsiders or "profanes", we Freemasons are a group of weird and secretive people that they will not trust. Sometimes it stems from religious indoctrination; others, from sheer ignorance. This gives us a very good reason to develop Lodge-community activities. We need to educate the broader community about what The Craft really is. By offering Library presentations about Freemasonry, open to the public, we may be working toward such objective.

Brothers interested in volunteering to present a topic, appropriate for such open activity, of about half an hour long, please join our Lodge-Community Zoom meetings, or contact me at [e-mail redacted] with its title and a brief description. We must attempt to give our first presentation in the near future, so current Library, and Grand Lodge enthusiasm does, not wane.

Finally, our Presidential Election is over. We have both, a new President (Trump) as well as a divided country. This difficult situation creates an opportunity for The Craft, that we should be ready to seize. I always remember (and warmly admire) Bro. Benjamin Franklin, who once said, during similar divided times: "either we hang together, or we hang separately".

Freemasonry is the Institution of Brotherly Love. We preach, and stand for Love of Country, Service to Humanity, and Tolerance. They are not just nice mottos, but important values that we Masons live by. There is much need for all these virtues, out there. By sharing them with others, in the broader community, we will be contributing to both, our country and our Institution.

Jorge L. Romeu
Onondaga District Mentoring Chair

The Mentoring Corner

December 2024

Hello, Brethren:

As I am writing this column, the year 2024 is coming to and end. By the time you read it, the year 2025 will be starting. In a personal dimension, 2024 has been a tough year for my family: serious accidents and sickness. And the world has not had it easier, either: wars, floodings, famines, etc.. So, we are all looking forward to a kinder, gentler 2025, and beyond.

But the sun rises every day, and God smiles at us in different ways, if we want to see it. The nice things of life are always at our disposal; we just have to take them. Concerning bad things, we can say, like old Job scratching with his tile: God giveth; God taketh away. Blessed be God.

There is a topic I want to revisit: the state of *The Word*. I have written before about our big problems, and about possible ways to fix them. To accomplish that, we need to realize that this newspaper is the work of all: both readers and writers. No single-man approach will help fix it.

There is a small group that leads the effort: our editor, the exec director, and several other volunteers, supported by our executive committee. We deal with crucial administrative parts: billing, collecting, paying, updating customer accounts, distributing copies, and so on. Much effort has been dedicated to modernizing the bookkeeping, using software. But much needs to be done, still. We had a board meeting this month, and we are moving in that direction.

The other component of *The Word* are Lodge Masters and other Masonic body leaders, who write their monthly articles. Sometimes, they do not send their articles and that is bad. Please, if you cannot do it, deputize your Senior or Junior Warden, or some other Line member. We need those monthly articles. These are not too difficult to write; just tell us what your Lodge is doing.

Then, we have the readers: without them, there is no paper! In this column we have said how you can find out what is going on in your own Lodge, other ones, and even in our neighboring Districts. There are also nice articles that our Editor selects from *The Builder*, which can also be discussed in open Lodge, since everyone receives the paper and can prepare for the discussion.

Sometimes I get disheartened. We printed a readership survey last year, to find out which of the word articles were most read, and which ones were not. We got back only 40 surveys, out of about 2000 subscribers. I am not sure whether our readers were too busy to fill them up and send them back, or if they read the paper, and saw the survey we had published.

Then, there is the issue of hard copy versus digital newspaper. Each hard copy costs us to print and mail. And, if returned for the wrong address, we pay for mailing it back. With a Digital format, we don't need to print nor mail the paper, thus saving substantial money. Still, most of our readers still request hard copies. We need more of them to choose the digital version!

The two killing costs are mailing and printing. The newspaper is being produced at a loss, and this situation cannot continue. We have a few alternatives, and neither of them is very good. If we continue as is, we go under in a short time. We can raise the subscription or create a two-tier subscription: one for digital, and another, higher, for hard copy. Or we can just eliminate the printing altogether and publish a digital or a web version. This latter option may not be the one preferred by some of the readers, but it will ensure the newspaper's survival!

Surely, our newspaper is far from perfect, but criticism won't help us fix the problems. We have had several Zoom meetings, trying to find solutions to these issues. But it takes time!

Finally, I want to wish you all, and your families, a happy, healthy and peaceful new year!

Jorge Luis Romeu
Onondaga District Mentoring Chair

2025

The Mentoring Corner

January 2025

Hello, Brethren:

One of the best-kept secrets in CNY are the Masonic readings in The Work, each month. As Lodge Masters we agree to give a presentation in every meeting. These articles are excellent examination materials! We don't need to agree with their content; just consider them!

In the November issue, we read Let Your Loins Be Girded About, by Bro. Paul Clark. This piece discussed what could men of action, insistent on results, think about Masonry? What could they have Masonry do? How would they release and apply the forces latent in a lodge? A group has been discussing Lodge-Community activities in Zoom meetings, a new issue, for the past few months. The article encourages us to try new things and not to be afraid to fail. Some new ideas do not work — but others will! Then, it states the saying: it is easier to reach the top of the ladder than it is to stay there and applies it to Freemasonry development. The author states: the problem is diffusing more real light in Masonry and teaching the application of Masonic teachings. Then adds: lodges devote too large a percentage of their available time to Symbolism and Ritualistic Masonry. And also states: The best Masonic idealism is expressed in its works.

Then, he gives a key assertion: There are as many different shades of Masonry in a lodge as there are members: each Mason has a different conception of what it means to him. Freemasonry is a big-tent organization. Some join because of ritual, others because of its history, others for its fellowship and its contacts. Some may want to join an organization, bigger than themselves. If they don't find what they were looking for, it is very likely that they will not stay long in it.

The author states: An opportunity for real service is given to every Master Mason who can get the vision for this great possibility. Then he adds: We need something more than just routine labor — Masonry is starving for brain work. Then, the author writes: Our public schools, revision of our judiciary system, or the proposed amendment to the Federal Constitution relating to child labor are but a few of the problems which confront us as citizens, then stating that Freemasonry must fish or cut bait! And summarizes his thoughts with: If the Craft can interpret its Masonic teachings in terms of real life, there isn't a problem confronting us which it couldn't solve.

There is a second article, extracted from The Builder: An Address to Candidate About to Receive the Apprentice Degree, which could be given to read to our new members. It presents the question: What then is Freemasonry? The rest of the article answer this, starting by: Masonry looks out on a world torn and bleeding from continuous conflict (...) The work of Masonry is to better these unhappy conditions of life. Then adding: The most important Petition statement is your avowed wish to be serviceable to your fellowmen. And thus, continues with these issues.

There are two other thought-provoking articles, also taken from *The Builder: an Editorial On the Interpretation of Masonic Symbols and The Lodge as a Community Center*. About the former, our own Editor states: This is something many of us have proposed for years. Wouldn't it be great if someone could look back from another hundred and say, "Whoa, look at what those guys did in 2024!"? Regarding the second article, this is precisely what our group, considering Lodge-Community activities has been pondering, all along. The article presents some concrete ideas: Why should it not make its own auditorium available for general public purposes? plan lectures and entertainment courses through the winter? equip a room which, might be used as a club by local men and boys? These are provoking thoughts that bring up lively Lodge discussions!

Jorge Luis Romeu
Onondaga District Mentoring Chair

The Mentoring Corner

February 2025

Hello, Brethren:

We just witnessed a peaceful government transfer: we have a new President and Congress. Transfers are the most important features of a political system, for they establish the successor. In countries ruled by autocrats, these govern until they die, or are deposed by another autocrat! In the US, if people don't like election results, they wait four years and try again. The stability such system fosters has made it possible for the American republic to last 250 years!

However, we still remain seriously divided. Some still view political competitors as enemies and their ideas as threats and dangers to our system. The media is analogously divided, and it contributes significantly to said discord. Such disharmony only hinders the country. Civil society including Freemasons, can work toward improving said social harmony by providing venues and by sponsoring respectful and open discussions of the major issues, between differing groups.

Another issue: at *The Word*, we have been working hard to save our Masonic newspaper. We believe that it greatly increases interactions among Brethren, Lodges and Districts. We believe that future Masonic researchers will examine our newspaper, to learn what Masons were doing during these uncertain times. Perhaps more importantly, *The Word* represents the independent and locally own and operated American newspaper; an endangered species rapidly disappearing.

The current issue of *The Word* has the Ad: *300 Years of Freemasonry: Its impact on Civil Society*. It has a link to its one-hour-long Livingston Library presentation, available in the web: https://www.youtube.com/watch?v=31rUnNsOIfk&t=1999s Its Power Point version is in the web https://web.cortland.edu/romeu/AnnivMasonsLivLibGLNY2018.pdf Both discuss the new and revolutionary ideas that our Institution brought forth in the XVIII Century England: religious tolerance, evaluation on merit, instead of on class or wealth, election (instead of heritage) of the leadership, and democratic operating rules, among other ground-breaking ideas for their times.

The Craft was a school of leaders, who participated in civil life without taking a partisan side (the Ancient Landmarks does not allow this). The Craft provided a forum for candid discussion. It still has a role to play: to soothe attitudes, to clarify arguments and convince divergent sides to debate them, publicly and with civility. We are the institution of brotherly love and tolerance!

This is what we have been considering in our Lodge-Community Zoom meetings: how to enhance further our current interactions. Our Lodges have always done things for the community such as blood drives, food collection for pantries, Christmas and Easter events for children. Also social projects, such as building ramps for the disabled. But in our Lodge-Community Activities Zooms we are talking about contributing to help lower the current levels of political disagreement by providing Lodge premises and conducting meetings that foster open and civil discussions.

We finish with a more orthodox topic: we presented a District-wide NorthStar project Zoom workshop to all Onondaga District Lodge Masters and Secretaries. For those unable to attend it, we emailed a PowerPoint with the main points of the program. The two most salient issues are: (1) NorthStar is not a strait jacket, but a framework that you adapt to your style and Candidate; and that (2) NorthStar's main purpose is to clarify to Candidates what we are and what we are not, and to assess whether such Candidates can become good Lodge Brothers. This exercise saves a lot of time and effort, both for Candidates and Lodge officers. NorthStar will help ensure that the new Candidates not only join us, but remain in our organization for the duration.

Jorge Luis Romeu
Onondaga District Mentoring Chair

The Mentoring Corner

March 2025

Hello, Brethren:

I read with particular interest last month *Editor's Prerogative* column titled *Il faut cultiver notre Jardin* (we need to care for our garden). In it, our Editor explained how he is receiving a daily email from the *Empire Report*, a digest of New York State news that he hasn't subscribed to, or cares much about. This news caught my attention because I also receive email from another organization, CLG News, whose sources and backers are not known. And I wonder how many of our readers are also receiving such types of unsolicited information, via email.

In his article, our Editor also stated how said email outlet reported opinions on issues where there might be two sides to, something that also worries this Mentor. For, one characteristic of many of today's media news outlets is the one-sidedness of their reports. This compels readers to seek alternative sources, with different viewpoints, in order to get more balanced information.

For over twenty years I watched the evening show McNeil and Lehrer Report. I tried hard to establish whether they favored Democrats or Republicans, but never could. They reported news, and not their opinions. And when some judgment was required, they brought at least two guests, one from each side. I am sorry to say that I can't find anything like that, in our current news.

During times when society is badly polarized, partial reporting can be harmful. Most people do not have the time to listen to the opinion of the two major political parties. In addition, as both parties have moved to more extreme positions, a big vacuum has been left in the center. In 2024, a survey reported how 43% of the voters considered themselves as Independent, more than either of the two major political parties (https://news.gallup.com/poll/15370/party-affiliation.aspx).

But, why should all this concern us, FreeMasons? I will not repeat our Tolerance, or Love of Country obligation arguments. I will invite you to take a look at our Altars, during open Lodge.

There, we place the Three Great Lights of Masonry: the Volume of the Sacred Law, Square and Compasses. Upon them, we take our obligations as Freemasons, for our three main degrees.

The Volume of the Sacred Law contains moral rules that we use to govern our lives. We are free to choose which Volume we use: the Bible, Koran, Veddas, or other. The Craft doesn't tell us what to believe in; but it does tell us that Masons should believe in something, actively.

The Square is used to square our actions. This means, to implement the beliefs that we have espoused with honesty, consistency, and fairness. In short, it tells us to be true to ourselves.

The Compass is used to circumscribe our passions. This relates to Tolerance, if understood as how we project ourselves in the world. We may have a belief or ideal. But we must not shove it down our fellow men's throats. We are, instead, endowed by the Grand Architect with a sound mind, to express our ideas peacefully, in order to convince others of its values and strengths.

What we have been discussing in our Lodge-Community activities Zoom meetings is how, or whether, we should enact this.

We argue that today's missing piece is the lack of a public space where such open, tolerant conversations take place. We propose that our Lodges facilitate their premises, and serve, as independent and tolerant moderators, to encourage people to engage.

Onondaga DDGM, RW Bro Toby Shelley, wrote in his article of this month: "of late I have been suffering from the ruthlessness of ignorance orchestrated by a press with an agenda. Our Country sure could benefit from more Masons in politics. Our Masonic Ritual teaches us many lessons, especially how best to get along". Kudos! I can't agree more.

Jorge Luis Romeu
Onondaga District Mentoring Chair

The Mentoring Corner

April 2025

Hello, Brethren:

Last month, Syracuse was honored with the visit of GM Reuben to Crossroads United Lodge. The GM had visited said Lodge two years ago, while still a Deputy Grand Master. There is ample coverage of this important event in last month's issue of *The Word*.

It appears that GM Reuben likes Crossroads United Lodge, and we don't blame him. It has a beautiful building that we call traditional upstate. Such buildings are often in a highly visible site close to the center of town. They are in brick, with Lodge room is in the second floor, and social events in the first. Onondaga District has several such traditional Lodge buildings: in Liverpool, Marcellus, Skaneateles, and Tully. Surrounding Districts also have such Lodges: e.g., Phoenix and Homer, whose picture appeared in last month's issue of *The Word*. Scipio Lodge building is not only very old, but also has a very interesting history, about which our newspaper Editor can say a lot. Modern Lodge buildings, instead, usually have a single story, with Lodge and social rooms adjacent to each other. Some examples include Memorial, Fayetteville and Jordan Lodges.

Half a century ago we had more Lodges, and even two Onondaga Districts — today we have only one. There was a four-story Masonic building in downtown Syracuse, that harbored several Lodges, some of which no longer exist, as they tendered their charters. Others, like Central City, moved to the Fayetteville suburb. Others, as Liverpool-Syracuse and Crossroads United, resulted from mergers. The vacated downtown building became the Metropolitan School of Arts. Today, we have difficulties opening Lodge with the minimum officers. Such issues have prompted some Lodges to hold joint meetings, an option that increases attendance and raises sessions quality.

This leads to our next subject: resuscitating our traditional Masters, Wardens, and Deacons (MWD) meetings. Conducting periodic meetings is of importance to respond to such dwindling membership. District and Lodge leaders can get together and discuss issues of mutual interest, such as developing activities that enhance and strengthen membership growth and retention. This has been a key objective of our monthly Zoom Group: to Promote the Development of (more and diverse) Lodge Activities, especially those that are jointly organized with the Lodge community.

The good news is that, on March 27, a Zoom meeting of Leaders of the Cayuga Thomkins Masonic District took place, organized by RW Michael Miller and Thomas Ostrander. Several Brothers, as well as Lodge and District officers, attended the meeting, and discussed old and new ways of teaching the MDC and NorthStar refresher courses. Two Districts were not represented in this meeting. However, it was still an excellent start. We congratulate them for said effort!

As an example, consider this. Two months ago, this Mentor, the Membership and NorthStar Chair for his District, gave a Zoom NorthStar refresher for all District Masters and Secretaries. Only two officers attended it. The following week, a NorthStar Grand Lodge Coordinator told us that a new Candidate wished to join one of our District Lodges, but that said Lodge did not have a NorthStar Officer! And no officer from said Lodge had attended our Zoom NorthStar refresher!

Every Institution with dwindling membership tries hard to recruit new ones. But they should first work on keeping and improving those they already have. Overcommitted leaders burn out in time, and can't fully support their main projects and obligations. Finding the right balance allows leaders to fulfill their duties effectively, for a longer time. Less is more goes the saying. Efficient Organizations are just as good, as the leaders they elect and support to govern them.

Jorge Luis Romeu
Onondaga District Mentoring Chair

The Mentoring Corner

May 2025

Hello, Brethren:

Before we break for the summer vacation, I would like to share a few thoughts about some strong features of Freemasonry: Self-improvement, Fellowship, Masonic Historical Studies, and Service. Many Brothers joined The Craft, and remain as members, because of them.

When we join our Institution and go through its three main Degrees, we learn many valuable lessons from its symbols and legends. The working tools, especially the trowel, teach us to create and spread brotherly love. We learn that harmony is the most important requirement to keep an organization working smoothly. We only compete to see who contributes the most. We start our labors by invoking and requesting the Deity's assistance. And we pledge allegiance to one nation under God, indivisible, with liberty and justice for all. We meet at the level, and give no special considerations to wealth or class. We part by the square, with integrity, and we act by the plumb, with dignity. All the above characteristics surely constitute a great self-improvement course.

Fellowship is about interaction, within and without our Lodge, with a group of friends that we call our Brothers. In these days of extreme individualism, having such friends is important.

Masonic history, philosophy, jurisprudence, poetry, landmarks and symbolism constitute important studies that some Brethren pursue individually, or in specialized lodges and journals. For these Brothers, *The Word* publishes valuable articles selected from *The Builder* magazine.

Finally, Service is about putting all of the above tenets to work, especially within our local communities. Contributing to foster harmony and rational interaction among conflicting factions in our country, is a valuable contribution that will not occur unnoticed. Developing activities that recognize the good work and qualities of everybody, both friends and foes, promoting respectful and open exchanges of points of view, in particular of those we dislike, contributes to creating a community that remains cohesive in its diversity, and by extension, an equally cohesive nation.

By opening our Lodges to community activities that operate under our rules of respect and tolerance for the opinions of others, or by finding speakers that examine the concepts over which there is controversy because they are poorly understood, may help lower the level of disharmony.

We have many well-qualified brothers that can talk about different topics. Each District can create a list of such brothers, including a short Bio and description of their topics. At Investiture Masters take an Obligation to present, in every session, a talk. This feature fulfills it! We need to attract more community members to our Lodges, if we really want to increase our membership.

Developing effective community efforts requires frequent and connected activities, that have good promotion. For the latter, Lodges need to pool efforts together, exchanging ideas through MWD (Masters, Wardens and Deacons) meetings that organize said multi-Lodge joint activities.

During the last fifteen years, our Craft has lost many members to death and attrition. A Chart (https://msana.com/services/u-s-membership-statistics/) describes this story, in numbers.

Community Service might well be one of the best recruiting effort strategies we can pursue. Recently, MWGM Rubin has launched the Community Service Initiative. Through it, Lodges can receive Activity matching funds, up to $500, for Educational or Youth-focused projects such as a fundraiser, an award night, mentorship and workshop programs, which we have explored before.

By becoming an asset to our communities, Lodges may undertake both, a valuable service to humanity, as well as to our own needs. Men usually appreciate joining proactive organizations.

Jorge Luis Romeu
Onondaga District Mentoring Chair

The Mentoring Corner
August 2025

Hello, Brethren:

This June, I attended, as I usually do, Saint John's Weekend in Utica's Masonic Care Community. This is one of the best-kept secrets that Freemasonry has in Upstate New York. There, especially for those of us who do not have the facility to visit New York City, we see the Grand Line Parade, attend the exhibits and meet with Brethren from other Lodges (I meet with Brethren of the two Spanish-speaking Lodges in New York: La Universal and La Fraternidad).

This year, a Retention Training workshop was presented to NorthStar Chairmen and other District Officers, organized by Bro. Lorenzo Cesare. After a great Brunch, we started in a filled Fellowship Hall of the Administration Building, where we were reminded of one of our key tenants: the Task of Masons is to be a beacon of light in the world (or at least in our community).

The welcome speech was given by our Grand Master MW Rubin, who talked about his new program to economically support Masonic community activities, a topic about which we have written several times in this column and that we have discussed by Zoom with several interested Brothers. For, by becoming assets to our communities, we Freemasons can fulfill two essential objectives: perform a valuable service to humanity and increase our own recruiting needs.

Brother Bob Siebold then presented an excellent training PowerPoint on how to enrich our NorthStar and other recruiting efforts. He put together materials that our committee, organized by the Grand Master several months ago, had prepared. It was a wonderful presentation that Bro. Siebold is willing to give to any Lodge that requests it. The PPT includes a wealth of information and of Masonic sources that help enrich the experiences of the new, as well as the old members.

Said sources expand our knowledge of Masonic history, esoterism, ritualism, etc., using the materials from the Livingston Library, presentations from Craftsmen-on-Line, Masonic websites, etc. It would be excellent if each District could request Bro. Siebold's presentation, providing Zoom options to those further-away Lodges that cannot attend the central event.

Another issue that was discussed is the loss of members that Freemasonry has suffered. For example, in the past 15 years our Grand Lodge of New York has lost 45 thousand members. But these numbers alone do not reflect the real impact of Masonic membership reduction. In 1960, there were four million Masons in the United States. In 2023, there were only 869,500 Masons.

The US population in 1960 was 179 million; and in 2023 it was 334 million. We developed an indicator called effective Masons that represents the percentage of actual Masons, in reference to the potential number of Masons. In broad numbers, the total population is divided into 50% of men, and 50% of women. Then, out of the total men, about half cannot become Masons because of their age (too young, too old), or status (felons). This reduces the potential number of Masons to about 25% of the total population. Dividing the number of Masons by 25% of the population total provides a better comparison, when considering both, different states and different times.

In the US, the effective Masons in 1960 were 4M/44.75M = 0.089 (or 9% of men). But in 2023, were 0.869/334 = 0.0026 (less than 1%). In the past sixty-five years the American Masonic membership has decreased to 0.0026/0.0894 = 0.03, or to three percent of what it was in 1960!

Attrition, due to natural causes (death) is inevitable. However, it can be compensated for by recruiting new members, and by retaining the ones we already have. The second reason is more important. For it is irrelevant how many new members we acquire if we are unable to keep them.

Jorge Luis Romeu
Onondaga District Mentoring Chair

The Mentoring Corner

September 2025

Hello, Brethren:

This month, I intended to examine the organization of a High School writing competition. But a more pressing topic needs examination: changes in our newspaper *The Word*.

If you look at our EMESB newspaper banner, you will notice that there are new officers, and that the old position of Executive

Director has been eliminated. These changes resulted from a Board meeting we had at the end of the summer, dedicated to resolve the budgetary problems our newspaper endured. Said matters will be explained in a special section of this issue of *The Word*.

Our newspaper budgetary problems resulted from larger expenses (in printing, mailing, etc.) and smaller revenues — as some Lodges, and other Masonic organizations have, or will, end their subscription to our newspaper. We survived thanks to the generous donations of several Brothers and Lodges. But such procedure cannot become the regular way we operate our newspaper: it needs to cover its expenses! The proposed new operation procedure will hopefully achieve this.

Since some of these issues arise from decisions to drop our newspaper subscription, I would like to digress about it. Often, those Brothers particularly affected by the decision to drop are the winter birds, the elderly, and the shut-ins. For, said Brothers cannot attend regularly, and only find out what is going on in their Lodges and Districts by reading our newspaper. They can also read interesting Masonic articles, that *The Word* reprints from selected sources. We know this, because when we visited them in Christmas to deliver Lodge packages and gifts, they told us just how much they appreciated reading *The Word*, and keeping abreast of things Masonic through it.

On the other hand, these Brothers were unable to vote on the motions to drop *The Word*, or to contribute their opinions on this important topic, as they were unable to attend such meetings.

It is useful, when considering a decision, to look both at the immediate and direct outcomes, as well as to its ancillary ones.

The special needs of our elder Brethren should be considered, too.

The Word is also a recruitment tool. This Mentor became interested, and joined the Scottish Rite, after reading about them in our newspaper. And, most likely, I was not the only one.

There is an additional dimension linked to our newspaper, that we have mentioned before: its historical value. *The Word* describes the Masonic endeavors of a mostly rural, but intrinsically American segment of our society. And it has accomplished this, for about half a century now.

Two years ago, this Mentor authored a research about the official quarterly journal *ACACIA*, of the Grand Lodge of Puerto Rico, to CEHME, an international meeting of Masonic historians (https://web.cortland.edu/romeu/ProgramaCEHME-Ceuta2023.pdf). In it, we analyzed half a century of the *ACACIA*, by reviewing over 50 of its quarterly issues. We discussed what were the most important issues at the time, how these developed throughout the years, and who were the key movers and shakers in Puerto Rico's Grand Lodge, in its Lodges, and its appended bodies.

Who can assure us that some time in the future, other Masonic historians won't be interested in studying things Masonic, in this very interesting period we are currently living in our country? Who can assure us that they won't seek, in our newspaper, the necessary material to research it?

Leadership makes or breaks an institution. There are Three C's that define good Leadership: commitment, competence and collegiality. A leader needs strong commitment to work that hard; but he also needs to acquire the necessary competence to develop good plans and programs. And a good Leader needs collegiality, to lead by example and persuasion, and not by intimidation.

Jorge Luis Romeu
Onondaga District Mentoring Chair

The Mentoring Corner
November 2025

Hello, Brethren:

Time flies! We are already writing the last Mentoring column for year 2025, an exciting period indeed, full of interesting Masonic events, both at the Grand Lodge and District levels. Let's summarize a few of these events, and extract some useful lessons.

At the Grand Lodge level, we have had a very active Grand Master. Of his many Edicts, the one we like the most partitions the State into regions, and assigns each to a Grand Line member. This way, Districts in those Regions have a high-ranking Line officer to deal directly with: more efficient manner to work. Another important Edict deals with actively encouraging our Lodges to develop community-oriented activities, by providing them up to $500 to support said activities. To grow our membership, we first need to bring our communities and neighbors into our Lodges.

Then, we had Masonic gatherings that put in contact different Lodge and District members. We had the Saint John's Day in Utica, a great mixer of Upstate and Downstate Lodges, where an excellent NorthStar training took place this year. And we had the

District Conventions, where all its Lodges sent Reps to review important elements of our Ritual, and to refresh district relations.

We have, through the years, underlined the importance of Lodges working together, within as well as across Districts. It is very important to understand this issue, and to have DDGMs help and support for encouraging District MWD (Masters, Wardens and Deacons) meetings. In these trying times of member attrition, the MWD allows Lodge officers to know each other better and to propose, discuss, and devise innovative and successful strategies to overcome Lodge attrition.

In the past, Lodges had hundreds of members, and their meetings assembled several dozen. Today, some Lodges have less than one hundred members, and many meetings start with less participants than those required to fill all the main positions. It is not helpful to have our newly raised brothers attend such slim meetings. We need to deal with this lack of sufficient members.

Some Lodges have merged; others have closed and turned in their Charters. Instead, Lodges can hold joint meetings, and visit each other, on a regular basis. Speakers may be brought in, to talk about successful programs developed elsewhere. Visits to other Districts may be organized. Such effective arrangements can be established during the regular District MWD meetings.

But most importantly, successful Lodge-community programs can be coordinated, and then developed, in MWD meetings. Last month, *Mentor* presented a blueprint for developing a high school student writing competition. When Lodges had 300+ active members, such projects could be developed by a single Lodge. Not anymore; we need to put together several Lodges to run it.

Mentoring is composed of two key elements: *recruitment and retainment*. Especially for the retainment part, the development of successful activities is of importance. An organization has to provide a reason for its members to invest their valuable time in them. And people tend to remain in those organizations that enjoy a strong public image and recognition. Nice Lodge-community projects can be jointly planned and carried out by several Lodges working through their MWDs. By developing them, we will both serve our communities, and strengthen our recruiting efforts.

In yesteryears the Masonic Lodge was a community pillar. We want to be seen as a valuable member of the *civil society*, defined as the group of non-governmental or business organizations, such as churches, VFW, Rotary, that help examine and advance the best interests of its citizens.

I wish you all a happy Holiday Season, with love and care, and a fruitful and healthy 2026.

Jorge Luis Romeu
Onondaga District Mentoring Chair

Abbreviation Guide

AASR/NMJ - Ancient Accepted Scottish Rite, Norther Masonic Jurisdiction

AGL - Assistant Grand Lecturer

AQC - *Ars Quatuor Coronaturum*, the publication of the Quatuor Coronati research Lodge in London

Bro. - Brother; can apply to any Mason of any Degree or having any other title

CEHME - Center for the Study of History of Freemasonry in Spain and its former colonies

CIM - Confederation of Inter-American Masons

CNY - Central New York, which includes the cities of Utica and Syracuse

COD - Council of Deliberation, the state-level governing body of the Scottish Rite

COGMNA - Conference of Grand Masters of Masons in North America

COVID - referring here to Coronavirus "COVID-19" and the associated pandemic

CS - Candidate Selection Process; the first section of the NorthStar selection and mentoring program of the Grand Lodge of the State of New York

CSO - Candidate Selection Officer

DDGM / PDDGM - District Deputy Grand Master / Past District Deputy Grand Master

DGM - Deputy Grand Master

EMESBE - EMESBE Service Bureau Inc., publishers of *The Word* newspaper; pronounced "MSB" for "Masonic Service Bureau"

ESM - *Empire State Mason* magazine, the quarterly publication of the Grand Lodge of the State of New York

GL - Grand Lodge; may refer to an official session of Grand Lodge, usually annually in New York City

GLNY - Grand Lodge of New York

JW - Junior Warden

LSOME - Lodge System of Masonic Education

MDC - Masonic Development Course (Grand Lodge of New York)

MMRI - Masonic Medical Research Institute, formerly the Masonic Medical Research Laboratory

MW / MWGM / PGM - Most Worshipful (honorific used for Grand Masters) / Most Worshipful Grand Master / Past Grand Master (not used for introductions; ordinarily "Grand Master" and the years they served are said)

MRC - Masonic Renewal Committee of the Conference of Grand Masters in North America

MSA / MSANA - Masonic Service Association of North America

MWDs - Masters, Wardens and Deacons

NPD - Non-Payment of Dues, a membership status not in good standing

OES - Order of the Eastern Star

OV - Official Visit (of the District Deputy Grand Master)

PPT - PowerPoint file or slide presentation, or a file or presentation similar to such

PPGM - Past Provincial Grand Master, under the United Grand Lodge of England

PR - (1) Public Relations; (2) Puerto Rico

R&R - Recruitment and Retaining

RW - Right Worshipful, the honorific used to designate past or present officers appointed by Grand Lodge, such as District Deputies, Staff Officers, Trustees, and Grand Representatives to other jurisdictions

SW - Senior Warden

VW - Very Worshipful; honorific that designates past or present Assistant Grand Lecturers within the Grand Lodge of the State of New York

WM - Worshipful Master

Wor. - Worshipful; honorific that applies to sitting and past presiding officers of Lodges

About the Author

Jorge Luis Romeu is a Master Mason, Raised in Island Lodge No. 56, Havana, Cuba, in April of 1969. These were difficult times to be a Mason in Communist Cuba, especially for a young man. (See more information in his Web Page http://web.cortland.edu/romeu/MasoneriaPage.htm)

In 1980, Romeu moved to the US. The social and economic conditions of an immigrant, plus the differences between Masonic Rituals and language, made it difficult for him to join an American Lodge. However, he kept his links with individual Brethren and Masonic listservs.

After a long hiatus, where he remained unaffiliated, Bro. Romeu joined the Jose Celso Barbosa Lodge No. 106, in Bayamon, San Juan, Puerto Rico, the land of his paternal family, where he regularly visited his brother and other family members. He later joined Liverpool Syracuse Lodge No. 501, in the State of New York, where he resides and teaches. He is a 32nd Degree Scottish Rite Mason, with the Syracuse Valley, AASR/NMJ.

He is a Past Worshipful Master of Liverpool Syracuse Lodge, and Onondaga Masonic District Mentoring Chair, where he directs the NorthStar Program. In 2014, he started writing these articles in *The Word*, the monthly newspaper of the four CNY Masonic Districts, skillfully edited by RW Steven Zabriskie, of Aurora NY.

Romeu also researches the history of Freemasonry in the Spanish Antilles: Cuba, Puerto Rico and the Dominican Republic.

For his published work, Romeu was accepted into the following Research Lodges and academic organizations, where he has presented and published several papers on Freemasonry: (1) American Lodge of Research, NYC, and (2) Western NY Lodge of Research, Buffalo, both of the Grand Lodge of New York (GLNY); (3) Jose G. Bloise Lodge of Research, San Juan, Gran Logia Soberana de Puerto Rico (GLSPR); (4) the Correspondence Circle of the Quatuor Coronati Lodge, Grand Lodge of England (UGLE); (5) Centro de Estudios Historicos de la Masoneria Espanola (CEHME).

Romeu espouses an action-oriented Freemasonry, that puts into practice the Principles we learn in Lodge, for the benefit of the society within which a Lodge functions. This approach is normal in Spanish Antilles Freemasonry, where he was initially Raised and molded, and is aptly discussed in his Bedwell essay *What is the Purpose of the Masonic Fraternity Now and In the Future* (https://web.cortland.edu/romeu/MyBedwellEssay2018.pdf).

Find a list of his research articles and essays in:

https://web.cortland.edu/romeu/ RefsTrabajosMasoneria.pdf

Publisher's Note

These articles were written for a particular audience for particular purposes. As an editor, I try to honor that, being true to the style and tenor of the writer. Apart from a few typos, only a few adjustments were made in grammar or punctuation. The expression is somewhat spoken rather than formal or academic, and Romeu employs a liberality of italics, bold text, and capitalization to convey emphasis, most of which are here preserved or nominally adjusted. Other nuances that may be construed as errors, such as the occasional omission of participles, were not corrected but considered as linguistic mannerisms unique to the author's use of language.

Only certain standards were applied as a style guide for consistency, such as the capitalization of certain Masonic terms, books in quotes, articles in italics, and the use and form of Masonic titles. I beg the reader to blame and forgive myself, as editor, for any other transgressions.

This book title is published under the imprint *"cyphrGlyffe"*, used by Amorphous Publishing Guild for esoteric and Masonic works.
More information can be found at:
Amorphous.Press/cyphrglyffe

Another Book of Interest ...

WEBMASTERING THE CRAFT

Fraternity in a Digital World

Webmastering [noun] – The activity of aiding, organizing, or leading a group's communications and public relations in a modern way; serving by use of skills and knowledge of the digital arts.

Bro. Ken JP Stuczynski
2020 Edition

www.ingramcontent.com/pod-product-compliance
Lightning Source LLC
Chambersburg PA
CBHW070131080526
44586CB00015B/1643